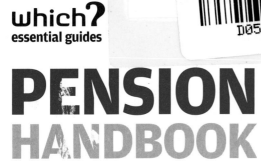

which?
essential guides

PENSION
HANDBOOK

❝ Your retirement is too important to be left to chance. Get interested, get involved and take decisions now. ❞

Jonquil Lowe

About the author

Jonquil Lowe is an economist by background, worked for several years in the City as an investment analyst, and is a former head of the Money Group at Consumers' Association. She now works as a freelance researcher and journalist and holds the G60 qualification required of financial advisers who give advanced pensions advice. Jonquil writes extensively on all areas of personal finance and is the author of several other books, including *Be Your Own Financial Adviser*, *The Which? Guide to Giving and Inheriting*, *The Which? Guide to Money in Retirement*.

which?
essential guides

PENSION
HANDBOOK

Jonquil Lowe

Which? Books are commissioned and published by
Which? Ltd, 2 Marylebone Road, London NW1 4DF
Email: books@which.co.uk

Distributed by Littlehampton Book Services Ltd
Faraday Close, Durrington, Worthing, West Sussex
BN13 3RB

British Library Cataloguing in Publication Data
A catalogue record for this book is available from the British Library

Copyright ©Which? Ltd 2006

ISBN 1 84490 025 8 / 978 184490 025 1

Author's acknowledgements
The author would like to thank Nick Kirby for tirelessly reading the draft of this
book and proposing as ever wise and thoughtful improvements.

Source material:
Barclays Capital: P.185; Department of Trade and Industry: P.28; Department for
Work and Pensions: P.16, P.17, P.29
Financial Services Authority: Information taken From the FSA's Comparative
Tables (www.fsa.gov.uk/tables) as at 20.12.05: P.67, P.111, P.159; Government
Actuary's Department: P.26

Editorial/design /production: Ian Robinson, Angela Newton, Paula Lock at
Which? Books, Guy Croton, David Etherington, Vanessa Townsend at Focus
Publishing

Cover photographs by: Getty/Photolibrary
Printed and bound by Scotprint, Scotland

Box: For a full list of Which? Books, please call 01903 828557, access our
website at www.which.co.uk, or write to Littlehampton book Services. For
other enquiries call 0800 252 100.

Contents

Introduction

Mention 'pensions' and thoughts immediately turn to 'the pensions crisis'. But the crisis means different things to different people.

Looking at the big picture, the crisis is happening because people are living longer. This means, if nothing changes, on average we will all spend more years in retirement and so the cost of our pensions will go up. The problem is exacerbated because the post-war baby-boom generation is approaching retirement while younger people are opting to have smaller families. It all adds up to an ageing population. The difficult questions for society as a whole are: how big will the cost of pensions become and who should pay it?

The government appointed a Pensions Commission (the 'Turner Commission') to look at the answers. It made two reports. In the first, the Commission gave a stark analysis of the choices facing society as a whole:

- Pensioners can be left to become poorer.
- Government can raise taxes or cut other public spending to pay higher state pensions.
- People can save more to pay for their own pensions.
- People can retire later to shorten their retirement.

In its second report the Commission came up with a proposal for tackling the pensions crisis. It recommended that state pensions be raised but to pay for the increase we should all work longer. In addition, people should be encouraged to save more by being automatically enrolled in a national low-cost pension scheme into which employers and employees would both pay. (The self-employed would be able to join too but without the benefit of any help from an employer.)

On the whole, these proposals have been praised as a pragmatic, integrated way of dealing with the crisis. But, at the time of writing, it was too early to tell whether they would be acted on either in full or in some watered down form. There are many fears. Some parts of government fear raising state pensions would add to government spending. Individuals worry about retiring later. Small employers wonder if they can afford to contribute to a national pension scheme. Some commentators fear large employers would take it as an opportunity to reduce the amount they currently pay towards their employees' pensions, and the insurance industry has the jitters in case it loses pension business to the national scheme. It could take a long time to untangle all these different interests and reach some kind of consensus. In the meantime the big-picture crisis rumbles on.

A crisis of confidence

For many people, the pensions crisis means a crisis of confidence. First there was Maxwell robbing pension schemes. Then there was pensions mis-selling with over a million employees persuaded to leave good company schemes and take out inferior personal pensions instead. Don't forget the near-collapse of Equitable which had some investors cutting their losses and has left others locked into miserable returns.

More recently, some of those 'good' company schemes have turned out to be not so good after all and are being wound up with gaping holes in their assets. Scheme members who thought they were on track for a comfortable old age have seen their pensions and retirement security being brutally ripped away. Even the schemes which are not going belly up are cutting future benefits and expecting employees to take later retirement. So it's all very well for governments to say: save more for your retirement. But is there any point? Where is it safe to lock away your savings?

Bad news makes big headlines. As a result, it's easy to get things out of proportion. There is no denying that some people have had a very raw deal from their pension schemes. But they do represent a small minority. Around 85,000 people have lost some of their occupational pension (in some cases a large part of it). But that needs to be set against the 10 million or so other people currently paying into company pension schemes who are doing pretty well. Of these, around 6 million belong to public sector schemes which should be relatively safe because at the end of the day the government can raise extra taxes to meet these pension promises.

The problem with pensions is that they are very expensive and, as people are living longer, that cost is rising further. It would be a tall order to try to save enough on your own over your working life to provide yourself with a decent pension. If you can join an occupational scheme, you get a big subsidy from your employer to help you build up that pension. In a traditional salary-related scheme, the employer has typically paid two-thirds of the cost of your pension; in other types of scheme, around half. This is why occupational schemes have been and generally continue to be, for most people, the best way to save for retirement. Although it smacks a little of shutting the stable door after the horse has bolted, the government has put in place a new regulator and new compensation arrangements to increase the security of occupational schemes, so hopefully the chances of another 85,000 people losing their pensions is now slim.

Individual choices

Unfortunately, there are other risks that you, the individual, are increasingly being expected to shoulder. The escalating and open-ended cost of providing pensions for an ageing population has become too much for many employers. They are seeking to contain the cost of their company schemes by moving away from promising pensions that are linked to your salary. Instead many are shifting to what are known as 'money purchase' schemes. This genre of pension scheme includes virtually all the personal plans that you can arrange for yourself – personal pensions, stakeholder schemes, free-standing additional voluntary contribution schemes, and so on – as well as many occupational schemes.

Money purchase schemes are, on the face of it, appealingly simple – you put your money in a savings pot, it's invested until you are ready to retire, you then use the savings that have built up to provide yourself a pension. The problem is all the unknown factors. You can't predict in advance how much pension you will get. It depends on how much is paid in, how much gets taken out in charges, how well or badly the investments grow and at what rate you can eventually swap your savings for pension. Two

people saving exactly the same amount can end up with very different pensions. One person can get a very different pension depending on when they decide to retire. With a money purchase scheme, you take on all the risks. So this is another reason why, if you have the chance to join an employer's salary-related scheme (still the most common type of scheme for public sector workers), you should normally take it.

To encourage all types of pension saving – whether through salary-related or money purchase schemes – the government offers a range of tax advantages. These tend to make saving for retirement through a pension scheme a better deal than most other forms of saving. And, bear in mind, that most alternatives to pension schemes – for example, saving through an individual savings account or investing direct in unit trusts – also effectively work on a money purchase basis, so do not offer any reduction in risk. Some jaded souls are spurning pension schemes and pinning their hopes on residential property instead. But banking on down-trading your home or selling up your one or two buy-to-let investments to fund your pension has to be viewed as a high-risk strategy. First you are putting a lot of eggs in one basket. Second, although property prices have risen fairly consistently for decades, the market in future could be very different. Factors that may dampen future house prices include governments' commitment to building more homes (in other words increasing the supply of homes) and the possibility of large numbers of unwanted properties coming onto the market as the heirs of the baby-boom generation inherit. While residential property might be a good idea for part of your pension savings, it makes sense to balance it with other assets and to choose a broad spread of different properties by, for example, using the new real estate investment trusts due to come onto the market from 2007.

Like so many areas of life, there is no totally risk-free path you can take. When you are planning ahead for retirement, you need to weigh up the pros and cons of different options and adopt the course which offers the best balance overall. By far and away the biggest risk to your retirement security is doing nothing at all – that's a sure-fire way of guaranteeing yourself an impoverished old age. The pensions crisis makes it ever more important that you as an individual take control of your retirement savings. You have a choice. You can passively accept a poorer retirement, or you can take action now to do something about it.

How the 2006 ('A Day') changes might affect you

More choice, less confusion

The Table on the right summarises the types of pension schemes which we will be looking at in Chapters 4 to 7 of this book. In the past, the tax rules often limited your choice about which of these schemes you could use. For example, many people in an employer's occupational pension scheme were not allowed to take out a personal pension as well. Since 6 April 2006 ('A Day'), the tax rules no longer restrict you in any way, so you can simultaneously pay into whatever sorts of pension scheme you like, as many schemes as you like and in whatever combination you like. However, individual schemes may impose their own rules – for example, membership of a scheme offered through your workplace will generally still be limited to people working for one employer or a group of related employers.

The new tax regime for pensions applies across the board to all registered schemes. There is no longer any difference in the way different schemes are treated. So, from a purely tax point of view, there is no difference between, say, an FSAVC scheme, a retirement annuity contract, an EPP or a personal pension. Some names, such as FSAVC and EPP, may disappear altogether since the distinction no longer has any relevance.

The main types of registered pension scheme

Type of scheme	Description
Occupational pension scheme	Scheme run by your employer. The employer pays towards the pension. Membership is typically offered as part of the overall pay package for a job
Additional voluntary contribution (AVC) scheme	Scheme offered by your employer which lets you build up extra benefits from the employer's occupational scheme
Free-standing additional voluntary contribution (FSAVC) scheme	Scheme you arrange yourself which builds up savings which can be used to buy extra benefits from an occupational pension scheme
Small self-administered scheme (SSAS)	A type of occupational scheme suitable for small companies, such as family-run businesses
Executive pension plan (EPP)	A type of occupational scheme suitable for directors and high-flying employees
Personal pension	Scheme you arrange yourself usually with an insurance company. Sometimes available through your workplace
Self-invested personal pension (SIPP)	A type of personal pension which gives you the widest freedom to choose the investments held in your pension scheme
Stakeholder pension scheme	A type of personal pension which meets certain conditions with, for example, a cap on charges and flexibility about when and how much you pay in
Retirement annuity contract	Old type of personal pension. Although you can still pay into an existing scheme, no new schemes could be started on or after 31 July 1988
Section 32 plan	A type of personal pension used to provide benefits transferred from certain types of occupational pension scheme

There will continue to be non-tax-related differences between schemes which are considered in Chapters 4–7.

Most people can save more

Under the new rules, there is no limit on the amount you can save through registered pension schemes. There are tax rules that affect you but, for most people, these are generous:

- You get tax relief on your own pension contributions up to a maximum of £3,600 a year or the total of your taxable earnings for the year, whichever is greater. You get no tax relief on contributions above that amount.
- There is a set allowance for the yearly amount you save (or the increase in your pension rights in the case of schemes that promise you a certain amount of pension) from all registered schemes. The annual allowance for the 2006-7 tax year is £215,000 which is well above the sort of increase most people will experience. If, however, your savings did increase by more, you have to pay tax at a rate of 40 per cent on the excess.
- There is an allowance for the total pension savings (or pension rights in the case of schemes that promise a certain amount of pension) you build up over your lifetime. The standard lifetime allowance for people drawing a pension in 2006-7 is £1.5 million – again, well above the value of the pensions most

people have built up. But if your savings came to more than this, you would have to pay tax at a rate of 55 per cent on any excess that you take as a lump sum and 25 per cent on any excess drawn as pension (which would additionally be taxable as income in the normal way). There is some protection for people with very large pension funds that are either over or likely to breach the standard lifetime allowance – if this applies to you, talk to a financial adviser.

See Chapter 3 for information about how these limits work in practice, and how the tax reliefs and tax charges are made.

Greater investment freedom

From 6 April 2006, there are fewer tax restrictions than previously on the types of investment you can hold in your pension scheme. Originally it was thought this would open up the possibility of using your pension savings to invest in, say, a holiday home, buy-to-let property, fine wines and other exotica. But, at the eleventh hour, the government backtracked and said you would not benefit from the tax advantages of pension schemes (tax relief on the money paid in and tax-free gains on investments in the scheme) if you choose these investments.

In deciding how to invest your pension scheme, bear these points in mind:

- **Your objective.** Make sure the investments you choose are suitable given your overall aim of building up retirement income.
- **Risk.** Unless you have substantial other resources, you generally can afford to take only moderate risk with your pension savings. This is usually achieved by having a broad spread of different investments. It would be very risky to have most of your savings in a single investment.
- **Tax charge** if you can personally benefit from the investments. If you or your household benefit from an investment held by the pension scheme – or could do so – you will have to pay a yearly tax charge on the value of the benefit you are deemed to get.

To take advantage of the widest investment freedom, you will need to invest in either a SIPP or a SSAS (see the Table on page 11). Even then, not all providers allow a full range of investments.

For more details about how to invest your pension savings, see Chapter 9.

Greater retirement freedom

Before 6 April 2006, many people were not allowed to start drawing a pension from their current employer's scheme until they had actually retired. That rule has now been abolished and opens the way to a much more flexible approach to retirement. Provided your employer and the scheme rules allow it, you could now, for example, cut back on your working hours and start to draw a partial pension.

Before 6 April 2006, you had to convert your pension savings into an annuity by age 75. Now you don't. You must still start drawing a pension by age 75 but you don't have to use an annuity to do so. See Chapter 5 for details. This extra choice meets the needs of people who are not permitted by the rules of their religion to use annuities and may also suit people who feel annuities offer poor value. However, if the appeal is the prospect of leaving a large chunk of your pension savings to your heirs, you may be disappointed as there could be inheritance tax on what you leave – see Chapter 8.

> ## Planning point
>
> You may have built up the right before 6 April 2006 to take tax-free cash from a pension scheme which comes to more than a quarter of the value of your savings. Provided the scheme has clear documentation to prove your entitlement, you will still be able to take that larger lump sum when you start to draw your pension. Get in touch with the scheme to check that its records are in order and ask for written confirmation of your entitlement. You lose the right to the larger lump sum if you transfer your pension rights from that scheme to another (see Chapter 7).

More tax-free cash for most people

In the past, some types of pension scheme were not permitted to pay out tax-free cash. This applied, in particular, to FSAVC schemes, AVC schemes started since 8 April 1987 and some types of pension used to replace part of the state scheme (see Chapter 6). From 6 April 2006 onwards, the tax rules allow virtually all schemes to let you take up to a quarter of your savings in the form of tax-free cash, though not all individual schemes will change their rules to permit this.

Planning for retirement

What are your expectations of retirement? For some it is a well-earned respite from the world of work, a time when leisure activities, travel plans and self-development can be indulged to the full. For others it involves living on meagre resources and facing a worrying future. Making plans for retirement is crucial, the earlier the better...

1

Retirement income

When will you retire? What do you imagine retirement will be like? Is it something you look forward to? Answers to these questions will be coloured to a large extent by the retirement income you expect to get and your likely expenses.

Having an adequate income makes retirement possible; it might let you retire early and allow you to enjoy a comfortable standard of living and do things such as visiting friends, taking holidays and pursuing hobbies. Having enough income might also be key in ensuring you control vital decisions about your well-being, such as having a prompt hip replacement or going into the care home of your choice.

This chapter looks at the extent to which you can expect to have enough to live on in retirement and how you can influence this by having a retirement plan.

RICH AND POOR

As the bar chart (left) shows, the financial experience of pensioners today is very mixed. If all pensioners are ranked according to their income and then divided up into five equal groups, the wealthiest fifth of pensioner couples have, on average, £924 a week before tax to live on. That's over £48,000 a year and enough to support a very reasonable lifestyle. By contrast, the poorest couples have only £185 a week (around £9,600 a year).

The picture is similar for single pensioners with the wealthiest fifth being nearly four times as well off as the poorest fifth.

A look at the sources of pensioners' incomes – see pie chart – reveals the main reasons for the big difference in the finances of the wealthiest and poorest pensioners. The poorest couples are heavily reliant on the state pension and state benefits. These

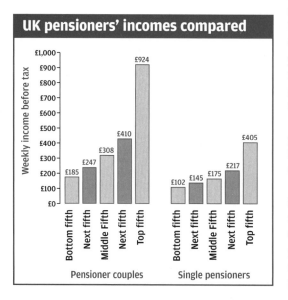

UK pensioners' incomes compared

Weekly income before tax

Pensioner couples:
- Bottom fifth: £185
- Next fifth: £247
- Middle Fifth: £308
- Next fifth: £410
- Top fifth: £924

Single pensioners:
- Bottom fifth: £102
- Next fifth: £145
- Middle Fifth: £175
- Next fifth: £217
- Top fifth: £405

Income sources of the richest and poorest pensioners

Wealthy pensioners have markedly different income sources
to those who are less well off

**Bottom fifth of pensioner couples
(Before tax weekly income: £185)**
1. State pensions and other benefits 81%
2. Occupational pensions 10%
3. Personal pension income 2%
4. Investment income 3%
5. Earnings 1.6%
6. Other 0.5%

**Top fifth of pensioner couples
(Before tax weekly income: £924)**
1. State pensions and other benefits 18%
2. Occupational pensions 37%
3. Personal pension income 5%
4. Investment income 18%
5. Earnings 21%
6. Other 0.1%

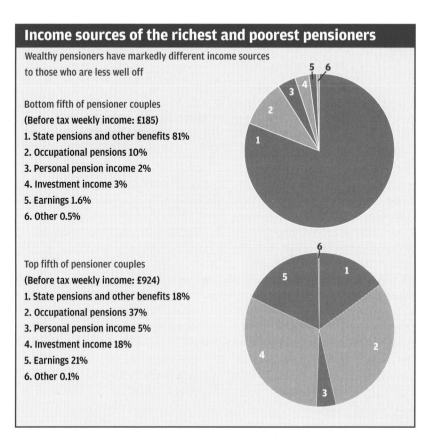

account for over four-fifths of their income and they receive only tiny amounts from other sources, such as occupational pension schemes. What makes the wealthy couples significantly better off is the substantial income they get from occupational pensions, continuing earnings and investments.

With single pensioners, the wealthiest fifth get over half as much again in state pensions and benefits as the poorest fifth and, once again, occupational pensions, earnings and

investments are the main sources of extra income.

The important messages from this look at today's pensioners are:

- If you rely purely on the state for retirement income, you are likely to be relatively poor.
- You can make a big difference to your financial well-being in retirement if you plan ahead by saving through a pension scheme.
- Carrying on some work can give a big boost to your retirement income.

Building a retirement plan

Building a retirement plan calls for a general review of your current finances and careful consideration of how you can build up your savings to generate the **retirement income** that you need.

There are five distinct stages to planning your retirement.

Stage 1 involves checking first that other aspects of your **basic finances** are in good shape. Planning for retirement generally means locking away your money for a long time. Once invested, it is usually impossible to get pension savings back in a crisis. So it is essential that you have other more accessible savings available for emergencies and that you do not have any problem debts that could tip you into a financial crisis. You must then weigh up saving for retirement against other goals that are, or may seem more pressing, such as making sure your household would be financially secure if you were unable to work because of illness or the main breadwinner died, saving for a deposit on a house, and so on.

At **stage 2**, you need to decide how much income you might need when you retire. You'll find more about this overleaf and in the remainder of this chapter.

Stages 3 to 5 are all about checking what **pensions** you have built up so far, deciding how much extra you need to save and keeping track of your savings as the years go by to check that you are still on target for the retirement you want. Chapters 2 to 7 will guide you through the process.

How much retirement income you want

Financial advisers often suggest you should aim for a pension which is two-thirds or perhaps half your current earnings. That's fine as a rule of thumb, but there are several reasons for taking a closer look at your possible income needs:

- You might spend a lot less once you retire, especially if you currently have a mortgage and/or children to support.
- On the other hand, you might want to allow for higher spending in retirement. This might be planned spending (on, say, foreign travel) or a contingency to cope with, say, age-related health problems.
- Your current earnings might be unusually low because of a career break or family demands.
- You might be earning a great deal now but be happy to settle into a less extravagant lifestyle later on.
- You might keep more of your before-tax income when you retire, because older people often pay less tax.

You can use the **retirement income calculator** on pages 20–21 to help you estimate more precisely the retirement income you might need.

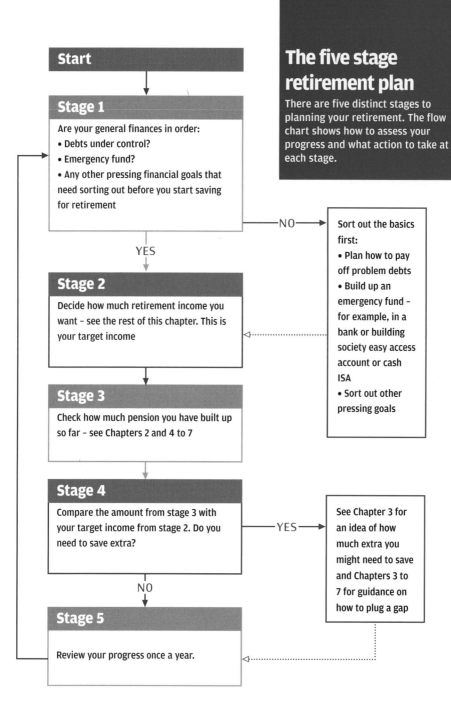

Start

Stage 1

Are your general finances in order:
• Debts under control?
• Emergency fund?
• Any other pressing financial goals that need sorting out before you start saving for retirement

NO

YES

Stage 2

Decide how much retirement income you want – see the rest of this chapter. This is your target income

Stage 3

Check how much pension you have built up so far – see Chapters 2 and 4 to 7

Stage 4

Compare the amount from stage 3 with your target income from stage 2. Do you need to save extra?

YES

NO

Stage 5

Review your progress once a year.

Sort out the basics first:
• Plan how to pay off problem debts
• Build up an emergency fund – for example, in a bank or building society easy access account or cash ISA
• Sort out other pressing goals

See Chapter 3 for an idea of how much extra you might need to save and Chapters 3 to 7 for guidance on how to plug a gap

The five stage retirement plan

There are five distinct stages to planning your retirement. The flow chart shows how to assess your progress and what action to take at each stage.

Retirement income calculator

Imagine you are retiring today. How much do you think your household would spend on the items listed in the calculator?

Day-to-day living (A)

This covers food, household basics, clothes and so on. Many are things you put in the trolley when you do a main shop. Look at your current supermarket bills: there will probably be just one or two of you in retirement so, if you are currently raising a family, you'd expect these bills to be less.

A £ PER MONTH _____

Household bills (B)

Allow for any rent to continue but, if you are buying your own home, you'll normally have paid off any mortgage by the time you retire. You might spend more time at home, which could mean significantly higher fuel bills. Council tax and water rates might be about the same, although you might save money by having a water meter installed. What about the phone? Many retired people are low-users. The TV licence is free when you are 75 or older. If you decide to 'downsize' to a smaller home, you may find that household bills shrink correspondingly. New appliances might be more efficient too.

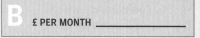

B £ PER MONTH _____

Transport (C)

You might save on work-related costs, particularly if you no longer have regular commuting expenses. You might decide not to run a car at all. On the other hand, you might clock up extra miles visiting friends. Bear in mind that people aged 60-plus often qualify for reduced, or free, rail, bus, coach and even taxi fares.

C £ PER MONTH _____

Hobbies and luxuries (D)

Would you spend more on hobbies? You may want to enrol in adult education classes to learn a new skill. You might take more holidays but these could be cheaper if you currently have to take them in the peak season. Would you eat out more often and perhaps go to the theatre and cinema more? You could qualify for pensioners' pub meals and concessionary tickets.

D £ PER MONTH _____

Health and protection (E)

Prescriptions and eye-tests would be free but not usually dental visits or spectacles. Medical insurance becomes expensive as you get older. You might save on life insurance premiums if there would no longer be anyone financially dependent on you. In later old age, you might need to buy in personal care which, at around £10 an hour, could soon mount up. You might need eventually to move into a residential or nursing home which could cost many thousands of pounds a year.

E £ PER MONTH _____

TOTAL MONTHLY EXPENSES (H)

Add together all the items (A+B+C+D+E+F+G) to give a monthly total.

H £ PER MONTH _____

TOTAL YEARLY EXPENSES (I)

Multiply your monthly total (H) by twelve to give an annual figure.

I £ PER YEAR _____

Saving, borrowing and major expenses (F)

You'll save on pension contributions and maybe other savings you make now. You might borrow less. But you'll probably still face occasional big expenses, such as a new washing machine or adaptations to your home. To cover these costs, aim to save a set amount each month to cover them.

F £ PER MONTH _____

OTHER expenses (G)

Add any other regular expenses here.

G £ PER MONTH _____

Couples

If applicable divide the annual amount (I) between you. Call the two amounts Ii and Iii.

ALLOWING FOR TAX

Before reaching a final figure, you need to take account of taxes payable on your retirement income. See page 22 for details on how to do this.

See page 22 for details on how to do this.

Notes
Use this space to record your calculations

TAX PAYABLE

You can't just set your retirement income target equal to your estimated spending, because most sources of retirement income are taxable. You need to have enough left after paying any tax to finance your spending.

Nobody knows how income will be taxed many years ahead, but it's possible to make a rough adjustment based on the tax system that operates today. Currently, people aged 65 and over get higher income tax allowances than younger people. And there is no National Insurance on pensions, savings income or, if you are over pension age, earnings from a job. This means an older person on the same income as someone younger often pays less tax. Based on these arrangements, the table below gives a tax factor for use in the retirement income calculator.

Tax factor (J)

Tax factor from table below

J £ _____

Couples

Look up one tax factor for income Ii and write it on box Ji: and another tax factor for income Iii and write it in box Jii.

Ji £ _____

Jii £ _____

Target retirement income in today's money (K)
Single person

Multiply your total yearly expenses (I) by the appropriate tax factor (J)

K = I x J

K £ _____

Couples

Multiply one partner's yearly expenses (Ii) by the appropriate tax factor (Ji) to give total Ki

Ki = Ii x Ji

Now multiply the other partner's yearly expenses (Iii) by the appropriate tax factor (Jii) to give total Kii

Kii = Iii x Jii

Ki £ _____

Kii £ _____

Tax factors

If after-tax income is within this band	To find the before-tax income, use a tax factor of
£0 to £10,500	1.0 (in other words no increase)
£10,501 to £17,500	1.1
£17,501 to £33,500	1.2
£33,501 to £44,500	1.3
£44,501 and above	1.4

The impact of inflation

When planning many years ahead, it is essential to take account of the effects of **inflation**. As prices rise over the years, the same amount of money buys less and less. For example, if prices double, a fixed amount of money will buy only half as much. The higher the rate of inflation, the more you have to save to reach your income target.

Some pension schemes give you automatic protection against inflation (see Chapter 4). But many don't and it will be up to you to decide what protection to build into your planning (see Chapter 5). The first step is being aware of the effect that inflation might have.

Fortunately, pension statements and projections these days must all be adjusted for inflation so that the figures you are given are expressed in **today's money**. This gives you an idea of the standard of living you might

Jargon buster

Inflation A sustained rise in the price level. In the UK, inflation is usually measured as the change in the Retail Prices Index (RPI). The RPI is based on the prices of a large basket of goods and services, typical of the items which the average household buys.

Today's money The amount of money you would need today to be worth the same in terms of what it might buy as a sum of money that you will get at some time in the future. For example £100 in ten years' time would be worth £50 in today's money if prices doubled over the ten-year period.

Assumption An educated guess which may turn out to be right or wrong.

expect and helps you assess the amount you need to save. To make the adjustment, the provider has to make an assumption about future inflation. At the time of writing, most commonly, future inflation is assumed to average 2.5 per cent a year. If inflation turns out to be higher, your eventual pension will be worth less than you had expected. If inflation turns out to be lower, your pension will be worth more.

Providers of non-pension investments (such as unit trusts and

Planning points

- Make allowance for inflation when you plan ahead.
- Plan to save extra if your pension scheme(s) do not offer any automatic protection against inflation.

 See the table on page 24 for help in calculating the long-term impact of inflation on future income and lump sums.

Case Study — Graeme

Graeme, aged 40, decides to invest £7,000 in a stocks-and-shares individual saving account (ISA) – see Chapter 3 – and set this aside for retirement age 65. The documents from the provider suggest that the £7,000 might grow to just over £30,000 over the intervening 25 years. That sounds like a tidy sum but Graeme realises it is likely to be worth less than £30,000 today because of inflation. He uses the table below to get an idea of how much less. He assumes inflation will average 2.5 per cent a year, so looks down the second column until he comes to the row for 25 years. He reads off the figure £539. This tells him that the £30,000 he might get in 25 years' time may be worth only the same as £16,170 today (30 x £539).

" Pension statements and projections these days must be adjusted for inflation so that the figures you are given are expressed in today's money. "

investment trusts) do not have to give you statements and projections adjusted for inflation. If you use these other investments for your retirement savings (or any long-term savings goal) you may need to make your own adjustments. You can do this using the table below.

Value in today's money of £1,000 you receive in the future

NUMBER OF YEARS UNTIL YOU RECEIVE THE MONEY	AVERAGE RATE OF INFLATION			
	2.5% a year	5% a year	7.5% a year	10% a year
5	£884	£784	£697	£621
10	£781	£614	£485	£386
15	£690	£481	£338	£239
20	£610	£377	£235	£149
25	£539	£295	£164	£92
30	£477	£231	£114	£57
35	£421	£181	£80	£36
40	£372	£142	£55	£22
45	£329	£111	£39	£14
50	£291	£87	£27	£9

The need to save

Retirement may seem a long way off when you are working but, for most people, it will be a large slice of life and it is essential to consider where your retirement income will come from. You will probably get some **state basic pension** (see Chapter 2) and this can be a good foundation on which to build but, on its own, is unlikely to be enough to fund the lifestyle you want. Therefore you will need to set aside some of the money you earn now to finance your later years.

Help from the taxman

You can choose to save for retirement in any way you like (see Chapter 3 for a range of suggestions) but there is good reason to choose a 'registered pension scheme'. Registered schemes include pension schemes at work (see Chapter 4) and personal pensions that you arrange for yourself (see Chapter 5). The government provides tax incentives when you use a registered scheme. These take the form of:

- Tax relief on the amount paid in.
- The money in the scheme grows largely tax-free.
- Part of the savings that build up can be taken as a tax-free cash sum when you start to draw your pension. But the rest must be taken as pension which is taxable.

Jargon buster

State basic pension Part of the state pension (see chapter 2) which nearly everyone gets.

Registered pension scheme A scheme designed to provide a pension and often other benefits too (such as life cover and pensions for survivors if you die) which qualifies for advantageous tax treatment.

Taxable Describes income or gains on which you may have to pay tax depending on your personal circumstances.

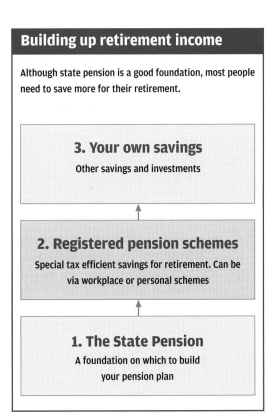

Building up retirement income

Although state pension is a good foundation, most people need to save more for their retirement.

3. Your own savings
Other savings and investments

2. Registered pension schemes
Special tax efficient savings for retirement. Can be via workplace or personal schemes

1. The State Pension
A foundation on which to build your pension plan

HOW LONG YOUR RETIREMENT MIGHT LAST

How long your retirement might last depends on the age at which you plan to retire and how long you are expected to live. The table below shows the expected length of retirement for men and women retiring today based on the average life expectancy of people in the UK.

The length of time for which you are retired has a major impact on the cost of your pension. For example, someone retiring at 65 with a pension of £12,000 a year who dies five years later will receive £60,000. But if they live to 90, they will receive £300,000. Whether or not you personally need to plan for this cost depends on the type of pension scheme(s) you have.

Some schemes, such as final salary or career average **occupational schemes** (see Chapter 4), promise you a certain pension for life. Your employer, not you, bears the risk and cost of you living an unexpectedly long time. However, you will need to think about the extra cost of a long retirement and plan to save extra if you intend to retire earlier than the normal age for the scheme.

With other types of scheme, **money purchase personal pensions**, for example (see Chapter 5), you bear the risks and costs. The longer your expected retirement, the more you need to save in order to accumulate sufficient funds.

How long retirement might last

If you retired in 2006 at this age	On average you could expect this many years in retirement	
	Men	Women
50	33	36
55	28	31
60	23	27
65	19	22
70	15	18
75	11	13

Women and pensions

Women pensioners tend to have less income than their male counterparts. In building a retirement plan, women need to consider what steps they and their partners can take to make their financial future more secure.

WHY WOMEN NEED TO PLAN FOR RETIREMENT

Women have a special need to plan for retirement. When the current state pension system was introduced in the late 1940s it was based on a model of society where most women married, raised families and looked to their husbands for lifelong financial support. The state scheme gave – and still gives – women, provided they are married, the right to claim retirement pensions (and bereavement benefits) based on their husband's entitlement. Many occupational pensions, especially in the public sector, follow the same pattern.

Society today is very different. Over 2 million women cohabit rather than being married. Nearly a quarter of UK children are being brought up by a single parent, nine out of ten of whom are women. And an estimated two out of every five marriages ends in divorce. This means many women, while still raising families, are not being supported by a husband. Also, married women who expect their husband to sort out the family's retirement planning may have their

> **“Married women who expect their husband to sort out the family's retirement planning may have their expectations dashed if the marriage breaks down.”**

expectations dashed if their marriage breaks down.

The state pension scheme has evolved a little over the years. In particular, since 1978 it provides

Jargon buster

Public sector The part of the economy to do with the state. For example, public sector workers are people employed by central or local government or state services such as the National Health Service. They include, for example, NHS staff, teachers, firemen, police.

Private sector The part of the economy which is independent of the state.

Longevity The propensity to live a long time. When longevity is increasing, people tend to live longer than in the past.

some protection for people, regardless of marital status, while they are off work caring for children or other dependants. This is called **home responsibilities protection (HRP)** and is covered in Chapter 2. At present, only 30 per cent of women retire with a full state basic pension, but the government predicts that by 2025 the proportion will rise to 90 per cent (matching the rate for men) as the full impact of home responsibility protection kicks in.

But the state system does not give unmarried partners the same rights to pensions and bereavement benefits as wives. Similarly, occupational pension schemes covering public sector workers seldom offer pensions to bereaved unmarried partners, though most private sector schemes do.

The problems for women are exacerbated by their longevity. As the table on page 26 shows, women tend to live longer than men. Therefore, many women end up living alone simply because they outlive their partners. Often the death of the partner signals the end of financial security.

WOMEN PENSIONERS TODAY

Today, nearly two-thirds of people over state pension age are women. Women pensioners tend to have less income than their male counterparts – see left. For a woman in a couple, this might not be important if her partner's income is supporting the whole household. But, out of a total of 7 million pensioner households in the UK, nearly half (3.2 million) are made up of women living alone.

The average income of single women pensioners tends to be low, especially amongst older age groups.

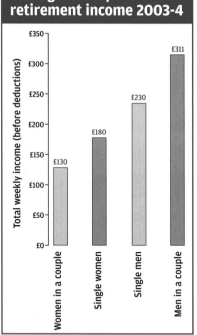

Average weekly retirement income 2003-4

Total weekly income (before deductions)

- Women in a couple: £130
- Single women: £180
- Single men: £230
- Men in a couple: £311

Home responsibilities protection (HRP) is available for those caring for one or more children under 16 or those caring for someone who is long-term ill or disabled. See page 41 for further details.

For example, the average single woman pensioner aged 60 to 64 has an income from all sources of £241 a week (£12,500 a year) but the average woman pensioner aged 85 or over has just £167 a week (£8,700 a year).

Looking at the sources of women's and men's income in retirement, the main reason for the disparity is that women have saved less whether through occupational schemes, personal pensions or other investments – see chart on the right.

WOMEN IN THE FUTURE

Although many social patterns have changed, it is still mainly women who take on the role of bringing up children. Surveys show that most women do not think about their eventual pension when making child-related decisions about work, but these decisions can have a huge impact on their retirement incomes:

- **Periods out of paid work.** While women are not in paid work, their entitlement to the state basic pension may be protected, but usually they are not building up any other retirement savings.
- **Part-time work.** Women with children often take part-time work to fit with the needs of their children. Most employers must these days offer some kind of pension scheme through work (see Chapter 4) and part-timers cannot

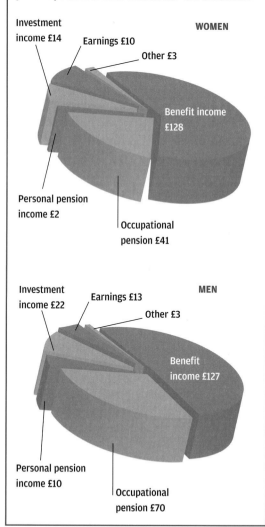

Where single pensioners' retirement income comes from

Looking at the sources of women's and men's income in retirement, the main reason for the disparity is that women have saved less whether through occupational schemes, personal pensions or other investments – see chart below.

WOMEN
Investment income £14
Earnings £10
Other £3
Benefit income £128
Personal pension income £2
Occupational pension £41

MEN
Investment income £22
Earnings £13
Other £3
Benefit income £127
Personal pension income £10
Occupational pension £70

be excluded, but part-time jobs are often in sectors or industries where the pension arrangements are poor.

- **Low pay.** The jobs mothers take are often poorly paid. If women earn less than a certain amount (£84 a week in 2006-7) they will not even be building up the state basic pension (see Chapter 2). On low pay, women are also less likely to feel that they can afford to make their own savings for retirement.

> ❝ Women with children often take part-time work in order to fit with the needs of their children. ❞

- **Impaired long-term work prospects.** Statistics show that women who have children generally continue to earn less once they return to full-time work than women without a family.

At the time of writing, the government had stated its intention to see what can be done to improve the pension prospects of women as part of its wider review of pension savings. At the individual level, women need to consider what steps they and their partners can take to make their financial future more secure.

Planning points

For women:
- try to build up pension savings in your own name that remain yours regardless of family changes (see Chapters 4 and 5)
- if you are relying on a partner's pension scheme, check your rights under the scheme and encourage your partner to make decisions which protect or enhance your rights (see Chapter 8)
- if you are going through a separation or divorce, make sure you claim a share of the family pension rights (see Chapter 8).

For their partners:
- consider paying into a pension scheme in your partner's name (see Chapter 5)
- be aware of how the decisions about your pension scheme(s) may affect her – for example, nominate her to receive any death-in-service lump sum, consider paying extra to increase a survivor's pension. (See Chapter 8.)

The State Pension

The state basic pension is the foundation (or first tier) of most people's pension income. It is paid at a flat rate to everyone who qualifies for the full amount, by virtue of their national insurance contributions, and at a reduced level to those whose contributions fall short of this.

State basic pension

The state pension is currently the only compulsory 'saving' for retirement that people in the UK are required to make. It is not saving in the true sense of the word since you do not build up a pool of money. Instead you build up the right to draw a pension in return for paying enough National Insurance contributions during your working years.

Pension sources

State pension is the foundation of your retirement income. On top of this you can build additional savings, through pension schemes and other investments.

Third tier pension

Other savings and investments – see Chapter 3

Extra contributions to second tier pension schemes see Chapters 4 and 5

Second tier pension

Personal pensions – see Chapter 5

Occupational pensions – see chapters 4 and 5

STATE ADDITIONAL PENSION – this chapter

First tier pension

STATE BASIC PENSION – this chapter

The state scheme works on a 'pay-as-you-go' basis. This means that the National Insurance collected from people of working age is used to pay the pensions of people who are retired now. When the workers of today reach retirement, their state pensions will be paid by the people who are then working and paying tax.

The state pension has two main components: the basic pension and the state additional pension. The basic pension is often referred to as a 'first tier' pension, available to nearly everyone and the bedrock on which to build the rest of your retirement planning. The state additional pension is a 'second tier' pension. Other second tier pensions are those from occupational schemes and personal pensions. Their purpose is to take you from a minimal retirement income to an amount which you might choose to live on. The third tier is made up of extra you opt to pay into your pension schemes and other savings and investments you earmark to top up your retirement income further. See 'Pension sources', left.

THE STATE BASIC PENSION

The basic pension is paid to everyone who has been credited with enough National Insurance contributions. It is often called a 'flat-rate' pension because everyone who qualifies for the full pension gets the same. But people who have a less complete National Insurance record get a reduced amount.

How much?

In 2006-7, the full basic pension for a single person is £84.25 a week (£4,381 a year). A couple, where each partner has built up their own right to claim a basic pension, could receive up to twice this amount.

A married woman can have a basic pension based on her husband's

State pensions and inflation

Your whole state pension (basic, additional and so on) is normally increased each year in line with inflation measured as the change in the Retail Prices Index. This ensures that the buying power of the pension is maintained.

Many campaigners argue that state pensions should be increased by the greater of price or earnings increases (as they were for a brief period from 1974 to 1980). Earnings tend to go up more than prices, so that people receiving wages and salaries can generally buy more with their money as the years go by and so gradually get richer. By fixing state pensions to prices rather than earnings, pensioners do not benefit from this improving wealth of the nation. Governments argue that restoring the link between pensions and earnings is too expensive.

Jargon buster

National Insurance contributions A tax paid by most people who work. There are different types of contribution, called 'classes'. Paying some classes of contribution entitles you to claim state benefits, such as state retirement pension.

Tax year A period of a year running from 6 April to the following 5 April. For example, '2006-7' means the year from 6 April 2006 to 5 April 2007. Generally, both taxes and state benefits are set in relation to tax years.

Working tax credit A state benefit for people who are in work but on a low income.

National Insurance record rather than her own. The maximum wife's pension is £50.50 a week (£2,626 a year). If the wife has reached state pension age, this pension is paid direct to her. If the wife is under state pension age, it is paid as an 'adult dependency increase' to the husband. This is reduced if the wife has earned income of more than £57.45 a week. Earned income includes any pension she gets as well as pay from any work.

If the wife has built up some basic pension in her own right and is also entitled to claim a pension based on her husband's record, she can have a 'composite pension'. This is made up of her own pension plus the lower of the actual pension based on her husband's record or the part of it needed to make up her composite pension to the maximum £50.50 a week.

> **" A first tier pension, available to nearly everyone and the bedrock on which to build the rest of your retirement planning. "**

EQUAL RIGHTS

At present, a husband can't claim a pension based on his wife's National Insurance record. Similarly, same-sex partners who have registered their relationship as a civil partnership can't claim a pension on each other's record. But they can from 2010 onwards where the wife or partner, whose National Insurance record is the basis for the claim, reaches state pension age on or after 6 April 2010.

Jargon buster

Working life The tax years from the one in which you reach age 16 to the last complete tax year before you reach state pension age.

Qualifying year A tax year which counts towards your state basic pension because you have paid or been credited with enough National Insurance contributions.

State pension age Age at which you become eligible to claim your state pension. This is currently at age 65 for men and age 60 for women. See page 53.

BUILDING UP BASIC PENSION

To get the full basic pension, generally you have to have paid or been credited with National Insurance contributions for at least 90 per cent of the tax years in your **working life** (see table, page 36). Each year for which you do have enough contributions or credits is called a **'qualifying year'**. 'Working life' has an official definition and means the tax years from the one in which you reach age 16 to the last complete tax year before you reach **state pension age**. If your state pension age is 65, your working life will be 49 years and you will normally need 44 qualifying years in order to get the full basic pension.

If you do not have enough qualifying years for the full pension, you get a reduced amount – see page 36. But normally at least a quarter of the years in your working life must be qualifying for you to get any basic pension at all.

If your own basic pension is reduced to less than the full amount, a basic pension for a wife (and from 2010 for a husband or registered civil partner) based on your contribution record is reduced by the same proportion.

Who gets it?

Over 96 per cent of today's single pensioners and 99 per cent of pensioner couples get some basic pension. The following people are building up basic pension:

Case Study David and Gemma

David has a working life of 49 years. But he worked in the Far East for a long time and has built up only 17 qualifying years to count towards his state basic pension. Using the table on page 36, he finds that the 17 years qualify him for only 39 per cent of the full pension. In 2006-7, this would mean a basic pension of 39% x £84.25 = £32.86 a week.

David's wife, Gemma, only worked for a few years before marriage and can't claim any basic pension in her own right. But she can claim a pension based on David's contribution record. Because he qualifies for only 39 per cent of the full basic pension, Gemma also gets only 39 per cent of the full amount a wife can normally claim on her husband's record. In 2006-7, she would get 39% x £50.50 = £19.70 a week.

- Most employees provided they earn at least a minimum amount (£84 a week in 2006-7) or are getting working tax credit.
- Self-employed people unless they have opted not to pay National Insurance contributions (this is possible where their profits are less than £4,465 for the 2006-7 tax year).
- People who are being credited with National Insurance, for example, while claiming state benefits during a period of illness, unemployment or maternity leave.
- People not in the above categories who volunteer to pay National Insurance contributions.

If your income is low

Under the current system, the government specifies a minimum level of income that pensioners should have to live on. If their income is below this level, they can claim pension credit (a state benefit) to bring their income up to that minimum. If all the income you had to live on was the state basic pension, you would be below the minimum and be eligible to claim pension credit. See page 48 for more information.

To check the number of qualifying years you have paid or been credited with National Insurance Contributions (NICs) contact the State Pension Forecasting Team on 0845 3000 168 or via the website www.thepensionservice.gov.uk

How much basic state pension you get

Number of qualifying years in your working life	If your working life is 49 years (state pension age 65)		If your working life is 44 years (state pension age 60)	
	Percentage of full pension	Amount in 2006-7	Percentage of full pension	Amount in 2006-7
9 or less	**0%**	**£0.00**	**0%**	**£0.00**
10	0%	£0.00	26%	£21.91
11	25%	£21.06	29%	£24.43
12	28%	£23.59	31%	£26.12
13	30%	£25.28	34%	£28.65
14	32%	£26.96	36%	£30.33
15	**35%**	**£29.49**	**39%**	**£32.86**
16	37%	£31.17	42%	£35.39
17	39%	£32.86	44%	£37.07
18	41%	£34.54	47%	£39.60
19	44%	£37.07	49%	£41.28
20	**46%**	**£38.76**	**52%**	**£43.81**
21	48%	£40.44	54%	£45.50
22	50%	£42.13	57%	£48.02
23	53%	£44.65	59%	£49.71
24	55%	£46.34	62%	£52.24
25	**57%**	**£48.02**	**65%**	**£54.76**
26	60%	£50.55	67%	£56.45
27	62%	£52.24	70%	£58.98
28	64%	£53.92	72%	£60.66
29	66%	£55.61	75%	£63.19
30	**69%**	**£58.13**	**77%**	**£64.87**
31	71%	£59.82	80%	£67.40
32	73%	£61.50	83%	£69.93
33	75%	£63.19	85%	£71.61
34	78%	£65.72	88%	£74.14
35	**80%**	**£67.40**	**90%**	**£75.83**
36	82%	£69.09	93%	£78.35
37	85%	£71.61	95%	£80.04
38	87%	£73.30	98%	£82.57
39	**89%**	**£74.98**	**100%**	**£84.25**
40	91%	£76.67	100%	£84.25
41	94%	£79.20	100%	£84.25
42	96%	£80.88	100%	£84.25
43	98%	£82.57	100%	£84.25
44 or more	**100%**	**£84.25**	**100%**	**£84.25**

Qualifying years

There are different types of National Insurance contributions and not all count towards building up basic pension. In general, only Class 1 contributions (paid by employees), Class 2 contributions (paid by the self-employed) and Class 3 contributions (voluntary) count, but there are some complications and these are summarised in the table on page 38.

For a year to count as qualifying, you must basically have paid a whole year's worth of contributions: for example, 52 weeks of earnings of at least a minimum amount on which

Planning points

If you are self-employed and your profits are low, think carefully before deciding not to pay Class 2 contributions. At just £2.10 a week in 2006-7, they can be a good value way of building up basic state pension.

you have paid Class 1 contributions (or are treated as having paid them), 52 Class 2 contributions, or a mixture of Class 1 earnings and Class 2 contributions covering the full 52 weeks.

Periods when you are not paying National Insurance usually appear as gaps in your National Insurance record and can reduce the basic pension you'll eventually get. But, in some situations, when you are out of work due to illness or on maternity leave, for example, you can get **National Insurance** credits or home responsibilities protection to plug the gap (see page 39). However, to qualify for any basic pension, you must have actually paid contributions (or had actual earnings on which contributions are treated as paid) for at least one of your qualifying years.

Jargon buster

Lower earnings limit (LEL) The lowest level of earnings which count towards the record on which certain state benefits, such as your state pension, are based.

Primary threshold The level of earnings at which employees (and their employers) start to pay National Insurance contributions.

Upper earnings limit (UEL) The highest level of earnings which count towards the record on which your state pension is based.

As well as State basic pension you may be eligible for State additional pension (S2P/SERPS). This is an 'earnings-related' pension which means that different people get different amounts. See page 42 for further details.

Which National Insurance contributions count?

Your situation	Type of contribution you pay	Details	Are you building up basic pension?
Employee earning less than the lower earnings limit (LEL) which is £84 a week in 2006-7	No contributions		No
Employee earning between LEL and primary threshold (£84 and £97 a week in 2006-7)	No contributions	You are treated as if you had paid contributions	Yes
Employee earning more than the primary threshold (£97 a week in 2006-7)	Class 1, full rate	Usually 11% of earnings between the primary threshold and the upper earnings limit (UEL) – £97 and £645 a week in 2006-7 – and 1% of earnings above the UEL	Yes
	Class 1, married women's reduced rate	4.85% of earnings between the primary threshold and the UEL – £97 and £645 a week in 2006-7 – and 1% of earnings above the UEL	No
Self-employed who has opted not to pay National Insurance (NI)	No contributions	You can elect not to pay if (a) your profits are less than a certain amount (£4,465 in 2006-7) or (b) you are a married woman continuing an election you made before 11 May 1977	No
Other self employed	Class 2	£2.10 a week in 2006-7	Yes
	Class 4	8% of profits between £5,035 and £33,540 in 2006-7 and 1% of profits above £33,540	No
Out of the labour market and not receiving NI credits	Class 3	£7.55 a week in 2006-7. Paying these is voluntary. You might pay them to fill gaps while studying or travelling, say. See page 46 for more information	Yes

National Insurance credits

In some situations you may get National Insurance credits which plug what would otherwise be gaps in your **National Insurance record**. You might get credits in the following situations:

- **At the start of your working life.** For the years in which you had your 16th, 17th and 18th birthdays if you were still at school and were born on or after 6 April 1957. You should get these credits automatically.
- **While training.** For the years in which you take part in an approved training course if you were born on or after 6 April 1957. Going to university does not count as an approved course. You should normally get these credits automatically.
- **When you earn less than the lower earnings limit** (£84 a week in 2006-7) and you are claiming working tax credit (or previously working families tax credit or disabled person's tax credit). You should get these credits automatically.
- **While temporarily working abroad** if the UK has a reciprocal agreement with the country in which you are working and you are paying contributions there.

- **While out of work because of unemployment or illness.** If you're claiming jobseeker's allowance or incapacity benefit - you should normally get these credits automatically. If you are getting statutory sick pay and the year in which you get it would not otherwise be a qualifying year - you need to claim this credit by writing to the NICO Contributor Group by 31 December following the end of the tax year in which you were on sick leave.
- **While you are on maternity leave (or adoption leave)** and receiving statutory maternity pay or statutory adoption pay and the year in which you get it would not otherwise be a qualifying year. You need to claim this credit by writing to the NICO Contributor Group by 31 December following the end of the tax year in which you were on leave.

Jargon buster

NICO Stands for National Insurance Contributions Office, the part of HM Revenue & Customs that deals with the collection and recording of National Insurance contributions.

 To contact NICO by post you should write to: National Insurance Contributions Office, Benton Park View, Newcastle Upon Tyne NE98 1ZZ. You can also call the helpline on 0845 302 1479.

- **You are a carer.** If you are getting carer's allowance you should get credits automatically. If you are a carer but not eligible for credits, you might be able to get home responsibilities protection instead (see opposite).
- **You are on jury service** and your earnings are below a certain limit (£84 a week in 2006-7). Applies to the years from 1988-9 onwards. You need to claim this credit by writing to the NICO Contributor Group by 31 December following the end of the tax year in which you were on jury service.
- **You are over 60 and under state pension age.** This applies to men (and from 2010 women) who have reached age 60 but are under state pension age and not paying

National Insurance or getting credits for other reasons. You do not have to sign on as unemployed to get these credits which should be awarded automatically.

> **❝Normally, at least a quarter of the years in your working life must be qualifying for you to get any basic pension at all. ❞**

With many of the above credits, you are not eligible if you are a married woman and you have chosen to pay reduced rate Class 1 contributions during periods when you are an employee, or not to pay Class 2 contributions during periods of self employment. This is because you are expected to rely on your husband's National Insurance record for your pension.

Case Study Clare

Clare left school at 18 and went on to university to study English Literature for three years. She gets National Insurance credits for the three years in which she had her 16th, 17th and 18th birthdays and was still at school. But the three years at university do not qualify for credits and appear as a gap in her National Insurance record.

To check the number of qualifying years you have paid or been credited with National Insurance Contributions (NICs) contact the State Pension Forecasting Team on 0845 3000 168 or via the website www.thepensionservice.gov.uk

Case Study Charvi

Charvi stays at home looking after her three children for 22 complete tax years, during which time she gets child benefit. She spends another seven years caring for her elderly mother. These years qualify for HRP. In addition, Charvi builds up 12 qualifying years while working. Normally her working life would be 49 years and she would need 44 qualifying years for a full basic pension. However, the 29 years of HRP can be deducted. Since 44 – 29 = 15 is less than the 20 year minimum, some of the HRP years are ignored. The result is that Charvi needs 20 qualifying years to get the full basic pension. She has only 12 qualifying years, so her pension will be 12/20th of the full amount. At the 2006-7 pension rate, this would be 12/20 x £84.25 = £50.55 a week.

HOME RESPONSIBILITIES PROTECTION

Home responsibilities protection (HRP) also helps you to deal with gaps in your contribution record. But, instead of providing credits to plug the gaps, HRP reduces the number of qualifying years you need in order to get any given level of basic pension. You can get HRP if you can't work because you are:

- Caring for one or more children under age 16 for whom you get child benefit.
- From 6 April 2003, a foster carer.
- Caring for someone who is long-term ill or disabled and various conditions are met.

HRP is only given for whole tax years (so, for example, where the child you are caring for is born part-way through the tax year, that year will not qualify) and only started from 6 April 1978 so can't cover any years before then.

The years for which you get HRP are deducted from the normal number of qualifying years you need. But HRP can't reduce the required number of years to less than 20. So you will need at least 20 qualifying years to get the full basic pension; if you have less, your pension will be reduced. From 2010, the minimum required years will rise to 22 for men and, between 2010 and 2020, will gradually rise from 20 to 22 for women in line with the rise in women's state pension age from 60 to 65.

HRP is available regardless of gender but, as women are most often the child carers in a family, HRP is especially important in helping to tackle the relative poverty of women pensioners compared with men (see Chapter 1).

Planning points

- If you are looking after a child for whom you get child benefit, you should get HRP automatically.
- In most other cases, you need to claim HRP using the form in leaflet CF411 How to protect your state retirement pension if you are looking after someone at home, which is available from pension centres and social security offices or the HM Revenue & Customs website (www.hmrc.gov.uk).

State additional pension

The state additional pension is an amount of state pension you may get on top of any state basic pension. Currently it is an 'earnings-related pension' because the amount each person gets depends on their earnings while they were building it up – different people get different amounts.

Who gets it?

The **state additional pension** used to be called the **State Earnings Related Pension Scheme (SERPS)** but from April 2002 was changed to the **State Second Pension (S2P)**. At retirement, you may get a combination of SERPS and S2P.

SERPS was available only to employees with earnings at least equal to the LEL (£84 a week in 2006-7). You could not build up SERPS if you were not working, for example, because you were long-term sick or at home caring for children or someone who was disabled.

S2P addresses some of these drawbacks so, from 6 April 2002 onwards, the state additional pension is open to:

- Employees earning at least the LEL.
- People caring for one or more children under the age of six for whom they are claiming child benefit.
- People who qualify for carer's allowance through looking after someone who is ill or disabled.
- Some people who are unable to work because of illness or disability provided they are entitled to long-term incapacity benefit or severe disablement allowance and they have been in the workforce for at least one-tenth of their working life.

Some people are not covered by the state additional pension, under both SERPS and S2P. These include self-employed people, employees earning less than the LEL, married women who have opted to pay Class 1 National Insurance contributions at the reduced rate and employees who are 'contracted out' (see 'Jargon buster').

How much is state additional pension?

Basically, the more you earn, the higher the state additional pension you can get. In 2004-5 (the latest year for which figures are available at the time of writing), the maximum a person could have was £140.44 a week (£7,300 a year). In practice, the high earners who would qualify for this level of pension have usually been contracted out for long periods, so the average additional pension actually paid out today is much lower.

There have been various changes to the additional pension since it was introduced in 1978, mainly cutting the amount of pension people could build up. People retiring now are still able to benefit from some of the more generous rules of the past. Once all the changes have worked through the maximum additional pension will be smaller but still in the region of £110 a week (£5,700 a year) at today's prices.

Under S2P (but not SERPS), in any year, people who earn less than a certain amount, called the low earnings threshold (LET), and those people who are not working but qualify for S2P (carers of young children and so on) are treated as if they have earnings equal to the LET. In 2006-7, the LET was £12,500.

Over a whole working life, this would qualify the person for an additional pension of around £60 a week (£3,100 a year) at today's prices.

When S2P was introduced in 2002, the government said that it intended eventually to make the scheme flat-rate with everyone who was in the scheme building up a pension based on earnings at the LET. It was thought that people within, say, 15 or 20

❝ In theory, the additional pension can give a big boost to your weekly income. In practice, most people get only a small amount. ❞

years of retirement would probably be able to continue building up an earnings-related pension but that younger people would switch to the flat-rate basis. It is not clear whether the government will press ahead with this change and, if they do, when that might be.

To check your state basic pension and state additional pension entitlement you can request a pension forecast from The Pension Service. Their website is at www.thepensionservice.gov.uk

43

Building up state additional pension

In theory, the additional pension can give a big boost to your weekly income. In practice, most people get only a small amount.

The method of working out how much additional pension you might get is very complicated and not practical for most people to do themselves. Instead you should rely on The Pension Service to work out your entitlement for you – see page 55 for how to get a pension forecast.

However, the chart opposite and Jo's case study will give you an idea of how much S2P you are building up in one tax year (2006-7). This can be useful if you want to compare the S2P you would get with the alternative pension you could build up by contracting out (see Chapter 6).

OTHER STATE PENSIONS

Some people who worked between April 1961 and April 1975 might get **state graduated pension**. This is an earlier earnings-related scheme. The maximum pension is fairly small – generally less than £10 a week.

If you do qualify for no or only a low state basic pension, you may be entitled to an over-80s pension from age 80. It is **non-contributory** which means your entitlement and the amount do not depend on your National insurance record. In 2006-7, the over-80s pension is £50.50 a week. In practice, any extra from the

over-80s pension would probably be matched by a decrease in pension credit, leaving your overall finances unchanged.

Case Study Jo

Jo belongs to the state additional pension scheme. She wants to know how much additional pension she built up in the 2006-7 tax year. That year, Jo earned £25,000. She follows the steps in the chart, right:

- step 1. Jo divides her earnings into bands:
- ignore the first £4,368
- band 1: £8,132
- band 2: £12,500
- band 3: £0

- step 2. Jo works out the relevant percentage of each band's earnings:
- band 1: 40% x £8,132 = £3,252.80
- band 2: 10% x £12,500 = £1,250.00

- step 3. She adds together the amounts from step 2. £3,252.80 + £1,250 = £4,502.80

- step 4. Jo reached age 16 in 1980 so (under current rules) her whole working life of 49 years is covered by the state additional pension. Therefore she divides the answer from step 3 by 49 which comes to £4,502.80/49 = £91.89.

The result tells Jo that in 2006-7, she built up £91.89 a year (£1.77 a week) S2P at today's prices. As with other state pensions, this will be increased each year

How state additional pension (S2P) works

By following the steps, you can work out how much S2P you are building up in 2006-7.

Divide your annual income into five parts as follows:

£_____

[A] The first £4,368 (lower earnings limit- LEL)

£_____

[B] The next £8,132 (band 1)

£_____

[C] The next £16,264 (band 2)

£_____

[D] The next £4,776 (band 3)

£_____

[E] Any remaining earnings

£_____

£A – IGNORE THIS PART as earnings up to the LEL do not count towards S2P

Multiply each part of your earnings by the following percentages:

[B] £B x 40% =

£_____

[C] £C x 10% =

£_____

[D] £D x 20% =

£_____

£E – IGNORE THIS PART as earnings above this level do not count towards S2P

Add the resulting amounts together
£b + £c + £d = £F

£(F) _____

Now calculate the number of years in your working life since 6 April 1978 (or the start of your working life if later) = X years

X years _____

Divide £F by X = £G (this is your S2P for one year)

£(G) _____

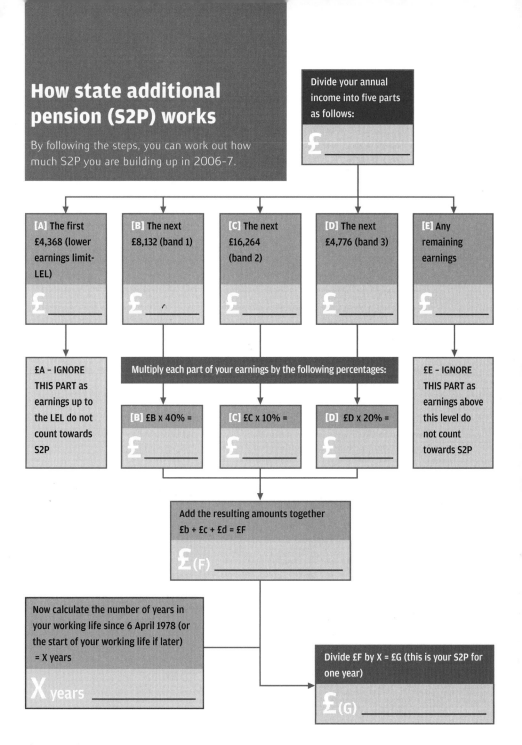

45

INCREASING YOUR STATE PENSION

During your working years and even once you've reached state pension age, there are steps you can take to increase your state pension.

Pay voluntary contributions

Periods of your working life when you were not paying National Insurance and did not qualify for credits or HRP will appear as gaps in your record and may reduce your basic pension. You may be able to fill these gaps by paying **voluntary Class 3 National Insurance contributions**.

You can go back a maximum of six years to fill gaps in your record. If you are going back no more than two years, you pay Class 3 contributions at the rate which applied in the earlier year – see the table below, If you go back further, you pay at the current rate for the year in which you pay.

Making Class 3 contributions can't increase your state additional pension.

You should automatically receive a letter from HM Revenue & Customs if you have gaps in your record, inviting you to make voluntary contributions. To check your state pension entitlement, ask The Pension Service for a pension forecast.

Making voluntary contributions in the 2006-7 tax year

Year in which you have a gap to be filled (in other words year to which the contribution is to be backdated)	Weekly rate	Cost for a whole year
2005-6	£7.35	£382.20
2004-5	£7.15	£371.80
2003-4	£7.55	£392.60
2002-3	£7.55	£392.60
2001-2	£7.55	£392.60
2000-1	£7.55	£392.60
1999-2000 or earlier	These gaps are too long ago. You can no longer fill them	

Is it worth a married woman switching to full-rate contributions?

Reason for the switch	Worth doing?	Why/why not?
To get more basic pension	No	Assuming you can claim a full pension on your husband's record, you would qualify for a basic pension of £50.50 a week at 2006-7 rates. The table on page 43 shows that a woman with a state pension age of 60 would need at least 24 qualifying years in order to get a higher pension on her own record. It's unlikely you have enough time left to build up a bigger pension
To get more state additional pension	Maybe	If you are an employee earning at least the LEL (£84 a week in 2006-7) switching to the full rate means that you would also start to build up state additional pension. S2P offers a particularly good deal for people on low earnings
To get a state pension earlier	Maybe	You might want to build up some pension in your own right if you will have to wait a long time until your husband starts to draw his state pension (since you can't start a pension based on his record until he does)

Married women who have opted to pay reduced rate contributions

Until 1977, married women could elect to pay Class 1 National Insurance at a reduced rate (or, if applicable, opt out of paying Class 2 contributions). Making this choice meant they stopped building up state pension in their own right and would instead rely for a pension on their husband's record (see page 33).

Although no new arrangements of this kind can be made, a woman who made the choice in the past can continue the arrangement indefinitely. Alternatively, she can end the arrangement at any time (and it automatically ends in some circumstances, such as divorce).

If you are a woman still covered by this, is it worth switching to paying full-rate National Insurance and so starting to build your own state pension? The table above considers the pros and cons.

See leaflet CA13 *National Insurance for married women* from tax offices and the HM Revenue & Customs website (www.hmrc.gov.uk) for more information.

Pension credit

The state basic pension on its own, even at the full rate is well below the minimum income that the government guarantees to pensioners. If this were your only income you could claim pension credit to top it up.

It can be very hard to save any money for a distant retirement if your income while you are working is low – other needs may be just too pressing. Even if you do manage to put a bit aside, the amount of pension you accumulate is likely to be small. A question if you find yourself in this position is: will your savings be too small to make any difference to your finances in retirement given that you may be able to claim means-tested state benefits? If so, then saving anything at all for retirement could be just a waste of money.

Means-tested benefits aim to top

> **" The savings credit ensures that even modest savers can end up with at least some increase in their total income. "**

up the resources of people on a low income. Since 2003, the main means-tested benefit for pensioners has been **pension credit**. The benefit has two parts: a guarantee credit and a savings credit. Depending on your circumstances, you might qualify for either or both of these elements.

THE GUARANTEE CREDIT
Any person aged 60 or over whose income is less than a set amount called the minimum guarantee is entitled to claim a top-up to bring their income up to that level. In 2006-7, the standard minimum

---

Pension credit and couples

'Couple' means a married couple, a same-sex couple who have registered their relationship as a civil partnership and unmarried/unregistered partners living together.

To claim pension credit you can telephone a special Pension Credit application line on 0800 99 1234 or visit the Pension Service website at www.thepensionservice.gov.uk

Case Study | June

In 2006-7, June has a state pension of £84.25 a week and a personal pension of £20 a week, making a total weekly income of £104.25. This is £9.80 less than the minimum guarantee for a single person of £114.05, so she qualifies for guarantee credit of £9.80. Her income is £20 more than the £84.25 threshold at which the savings credit starts, so she is also entitled to a savings credit of 20 x 60p = £12. The pension credit has boosted her weekly income to £104.25 + £9.80 + £12 = £126.05.

guarantee is £114.05 a week for a single person and £174.05 for a couple. The minimum guarantee is higher for those people who are severely disabled and for carers, and can include extra to cover some housing costs.

Under the current rules, the minimum guarantee is increased each year in line with national average earnings.

THE SAVINGS CREDIT

A problem inherent in the guarantee credit is that it discourages people who do not expect to have much income in retirement from saving anything at all. What is the point of saving enough to provide, say, £20 a week in retirement if it will simply replace money you could otherwise have claimed through the guarantee credit? To tackle this problem, pension credit also has a savings credit which is designed to reward you for making your own savings for retirement.

If you are aged 65 or over, you can claim a savings credit of 60p for each £1 of income that you have between two thresholds. The lower threshold at which savings credit starts is the same as the maximum state basic retirement pension (£84.25 a week for a single person and £134.75 for a couple in 2006-7). The upper threshold is the minimum guarantee described above (£114.05 a week for a single person and £174.05 for a couple in 2006-7). In 2006-7, this gives a maximum savings credit of £17.88 a week if you are single and £23.58 if you are a couple.

The savings credit is reduced by 40p for each £1 of income above the minimum guarantee. In this way, the savings credit is tapered away to nothing for single people with income of £158.75 or more and couples with income of £233.00 or more. The tables on the next two pages give examples of how much you can get depending on your retirement income.

IS PENSION CREDIT A BARRIER TO SAVING FOR RETIREMENT?

Most financial advisers will not recommend that people on low incomes make any pension savings for retirement. The advisers are fearful that they may be accused of mis-selling to people who could not gain from saving if the retirement income produced is merely offset by means-tested benefits.

If the pension credit had just the guarantee element, then any savings which failed to take your income over the minimum guarantee would indeed be wasted. The savings credit was introduced specifically to tackle this problem. It ensures that modest savers end up with at least some increase in their total income as a result of saving. But is the increase enough? Consider the case study on page 49. June had saved enough to produce a pension of £20 a week but her income after benefits was just £12 higher than if she had made no savings at all. It's the same effect as

Examples of pension credit for a single pensioner

To see how pension credit boosts retirement income in 2006-7, compare the figure in the left hand column with that in the column on the far right.

Your income from all sources	Income above threshold at which savings credit starts	Guarantee credit	Savings credit	Your income including pension credit
£50	£0	£64.05	£0.00	£114.05
£60	£0	£54.05	£0.00	£114.05
£70	£0	£44.05	£0.00	£114.05
£84.25 [1]	£0	£29.80	£0.00	£114.05
£90	£5.75	£24.05	£3.45	£117.50
£100	£15.75	£14.05	£9.45	£123.50
£114.05 [2]	£29.80	£0.00	£17.88	£131.93
£120	£35.75	£0.00	£15.50	£135.50
£130	£45.75	£0.00	£11.50	£141.50
£140	£55.75	£0.00	£7.50	£147.50
£150	£65.75	£0.00	£3.50	£153.50
£158.75 [3]	£74.50	£0.00	£0.00	£158.75

1 Threshold at which savings credit starts (equal to full state basic pension). 2 Minimum guarantee (and threshold at which savings credit starts to be lost). 3 Income level at which all savings credit lost.

Examples of pension credit for a pensioner couple

To see how pension credit boosts a couple's retirement income compare the figure in the left-hand column with that in column on the far right.

Your income from all sources	Income above threshold at which savings credit starts	Guarantee credit	Savings credit	Your income including pension credit
£50	£0	£124.05	£0.00	£174.05
£60	£0	£114.05	£0.00	£174.05
£70	£0	£104.05	£0.00	£174.05
£80	£0	£94.05	£0.00	£174.05
£90	£0	£84.05	£0.00	£174.05
£100	£0	£74.05	£0.00	£174.05
£110	£0	£64.05	£0.00	£174.05
£120	£0	£54.05	£0.00	£174.05
£134.75 [1]	£0	£39.30	£0.00	£174.05
£140	£5.25	£34.05	£3.15	£177.20
£150	£15.25	£24.05	£9.15	£183.20
£160	£25.25	£14.05	£15.15	£189.20
£170	£35.25	£4.05	£21.15	£195.20
£174.05 [2]	£39.30	£0.00	£23.58	£197.63
£180	£45.25	£0.00	£21.20	£201.20
£190	£55.25	£0.00	£17.20	£207.20
£200	£65.25	£0.00	£13.20	£213.20
£210	£75.25	£0.00	£9.20	£219.20
£220	£85.25	£0.00	£5.20	£225.20
£233.00 [3]	£98.25	£0.00	£0.00	£233.00

1 Threshold at which savings credit starts (equal to full state basic pension). 2 Minimum guarantee (and threshold at which savings credit starts to be lost). 3 Income level at which all savings credit lost.

if she had been taxed £8 on her pension of £20 – equivalent to a 40 per cent tax rate.

On its own, a 40 per cent tax charge on savings might well discourage people from saving for retirement. But there is a further drawback as well. If you are many years from retirement, what elements of the state system can you rely on to be around when you retire? Is the savings credit – which was introduced to tackle the poverty of today's pensioners - likely to continue into the long-term? If not,

> **"If you are many years from retirement, what elements of the state system can you rely on to be around when you finally retire?"**

small retirement savings could be totally wasted.

On the other hand, what happens if you make no savings for retirement? You are presumably banking on some kind of guarantee credit still being available when you eventually retire. This might be a reasonable assumption since modern governments tend to recognise a poverty level below which no citizen should live. But the **minimum guarantee** could be much lower than today. At the time of writing, there were rumours that the government might cease to increase the minimum guarantee each year in line with earnings from 2008. If instead it were

Unclaimed pension credit
Pension credit was introduced in October 2003. By the end of that year, only around two-thirds of the people who were eligible were claiming the new benefit. Between 1.26 and 1.84 million people were failing to claim the money they were entitled to. Of these, two-thirds could have claimed more than £10 a week – enough to make a significant difference to their household income.

Pension credit is not paid out automatically. It has to be claimed. This can be done by calling the Pension Credit Application Line 0800 99 1234 or by filling in a form which you can download from www.thepensionservice.gov.uk.

People eligible for pension credit may also qualify for council tax benefit and, if they pay rent, housing benefit. Both benefits can be claimed at the same time as pension credit when calling the Pension Credit Application Line.

Jargon buster

Retirement Used in this book to mean the period of life when you draw a pension. You might not have stopped work altogether.

Means-tested state benefit Income from the state where the amount you get depends on the level of your income from other sources (and, in some cases, also your savings). An example is pension credit.

increased in line with prices, although the buying power of the income would be maintained, the poorest pensioners would not share in the nation's economic growth and would become progressively poorer relative to the working population.

DRAWING YOUR STATE PENSION

State pensions are payable once you reach **state pension age**. The state pension age for people retiring now is 65 for men and 60 for women.

Women's pension age is being increased for women retiring over the period 2010 to 2020. If you are a woman, your actual state pension age will depend on when you were born:

- Born before 6 April 1950. Your state pension age is 60.
- Born between 6 April 1950 and 5 March 1955. Your state pension age is between age 60 and 65 depending on when your birth date falls. To calculate the age, take 60 and add one month for each tax month, or part tax month, by which your birth date falls after 5 April 1950. For example, if you were born on 5 May 1950, your state

Planning point

You can calculate your state pension age online using the government calculator at www.thepensionservice.gov.uk/resourcecentre/home/statepensioncalc.asp.

pension age is 60 years and one month and the date from which you can start to get a state pension is 6 May 2010. If you were born on 5 March 1955, your state pension age is 64 years and 11 months and the date from which you can start to get a state pension is 6 January 2020.

- Born from 6 March 1955 onwards. Your state pension age is 65.

The government appointed a Pensions Commission to review the adequacy of the UK's pension savings (see Introduction). One of its suggestions is that the state pension age should be gradually increased to, say, 68 by 2050 because people are now living much longer than they were when the standard age of 65 was first set. The government is considering the Commission's findings but will not necessarily follow its proposals.

You can't start to get a state pension before reaching state pension age, but you can put off the start of your state pension to a later age. In that case, you earn either extra pension or a lump sum. See page 54 for details.

Case Study Lesley

Lesley was born on 10 December 1951. This means her birthday falls 20 months and 5 days after 5 April 1950. Therefore she must add 21 months to age 60 in order to find out her state pension age. This comes to 61 years and 9 months. She can start to receive her pension from the beginning of the tax month in which she reaches this age which will be the tax month starting 6 September 2013.

> **"Where you defer your pension on or after 6 April 2005, you earn an increase of 10.4 per cent for each whole year. "**

Deferring your state pension

You don't have to start drawing your pension at state pension age. Instead you can defer your pension, in which case you earn either extra pension once it does start to be paid or a lump sum. You can put off drawing your pension for as long as you like. Any pension for a wife (or from 2010 a husband or registered civil partner) based on your National Insurance record must also be deferred for the same period.

If your pension has already started to be paid, you can decide to stop the payments in order to earn extra pension or a lump sum. But you can only defer your pension once.

Where you defer your pension on or after 6 April 2005, you earn an increase in the pension when it does

Case Study | Talia

Talia is 60 and could start getting a state pension of £50 a week. But she plans to carry on working for another three years until her husband also retires, so she doesn't need her pension yet. Ignoring increases in line with inflation, this would mean giving up three years' pension worth £7,800. At the end of three years, she might get a lump sum of around £8,590 (before tax) or alternatively could get extra pension of £15.60 a week (£811 a year) for the rest of her life.

start of 1/5 per cent for every week you put off the pension (with a minimum overall increase of 1 per cent). This is equivalent to an increase of 10.4 per cent for each whole year. The extra pension is taxable in the same way as the rest of your state pension.

Alternatively, provided you put off claiming your pension for at least a year, you can earn a one-off lump sum instead of extra pension. The lump sum is taxable but only at the top rate you were paying before getting the lump sum – in other words, whatever the size of lump sum, it does not result in you moving into a higher tax bracket.

KEEPING TRACK OF YOUR STATE PENSION

You can at a pinch work out your own entitlement to the state basic pension, but it's well nigh impossible to calculate your state additional pension. Save yourself the effort by getting a **state pension forecast** from The Pension Service (www.thepensionservice.gov.uk). Recently, The Pension Service has started to send out statements automatically, so you might not need to request one.

The forecast is in the form of a letter and it will contain information along the lines shown in the Box. Because your actual state pension will depend on what happens over the whole of your working life, the forecast can only be an estimate based on what has happened so far and assumptions that your present circumstances will continue for the foreseeable future. So the forecast is a useful guide to the state pension you might get but not a guarantee that you will definitely get the amount shown.

If you belong to an **occupational pension scheme** (see Chapter 4) or have a **personal pension** (see Chapter 5), you will get regular statements indicating the pension you may get from the scheme. In some cases, the statement may be a '**combined statement**' in which case it will also include a state pension forecast based on your own National Insurance record. If you do get a combined statement, you will not need to ask for a state pension forecast from The Pension Service.

Don't confuse an ordinary statement from an occupational pension scheme or personal pension with a combined forecast. An ordinary statement will often include a note of the full state basic pension that you might get at retirement but, unlike a combined statement, the figure will not be personal to you or based on your own specific National Insurance record.

What a state pension forecast tells you

State pension forecasts are sent out by the government. They show how much state pension you might get starting from state pension age given your actual National Insurance record to date and assuming your current employment situation continues unchanged. The forecast might, say, for example:

Your weekly amount of basic state pension: £76.02
Your weekly amount of additional state pension: £14.91
Your total weekly amount of state pension: £90.93

You can use the forecast to help you work out whether you are on track for the retirement income you want.

❝ The forecast is a useful guide to the state pension you might get but not a guarantee that you will definitely get the amount shown. ❞

If you belong to more than one pension scheme, you might get more than one combined statement. If so, make sure you don't double count your state pension when adding up your expected pensions from all sources.

For further details of the state pensions and benefits discussed in this chapter and National Insurance contributions consult the leaflets listed below. Many can now be downloaded from The Pension Service website (www.thepensionservice.gov.uk) and HM Revenue & Customs (www.hmrc.gov.uk).

Planning points

- Get a forecast of your state pension.
- Use it to help you work out how much extra you might need to save for retirement – see Chapter 3.
- Consider whether there are steps you can take now to boost your state pension – for example, paying voluntary Class 3 contributions.
- Bear in mind you may be able to start your pension later than the normal state pension age in order to earn extra pension or a lump sum.

Free leaflets about pensions and National Insurance

Reference	Title	From
CA93	Shortfall in your NICs; National Insurance contributions. To pay or not to pay?	HM Revenue & Customs
PM1	A guide to your pension options	The Pension Service
PM2	State pensions - Your guide	The Pension Service
PM6	Pensions for women - Your guide	The Pension Service
PM9	State pensions for parents and carers	The Pension Service
BR19	State pension forecast (request form)	The Pension Service
BR19L	Understanding your state pension forecast	The Pension Service
BR33	State pension - The choices available to you	The Pension Service
CPF5	Your pension statement (combined statements)	The Pension Service
SPD1	State pension deferral - Your state pension choice - Pension now or extra pension later: a guide to state pension deferral	The Pension Service
NP46	A guide to state pensions	The Pension Service
	Your guide to state pension deferral	The Pension Service

A pension gap

A pension gap is a shortfall between the amount you need to live on in retirement and the income you are on track to receive as pension. To close this you need to look at ways of boosting your retirement income. The sooner you start, the better your chances of success.

Plugging the pensions gap

From the preceding chapters it is clear that the state pension on its own is not going to be enough to support the standard of living most people want in retirement. In all likelihood, you will need to save extra.

A PENSIONS SHORTFALL

The Turner Commission (see Introduction) estimated that UK households have built up pension savings and pension rights in occupational schemes and personal pensions worth around £1,800 billion. That sounds a staggering amount, but, research in 2001 for the Association of British Insurers (www.abi.org.uk) estimated that the population as a whole is saving £27 billion too little each year to secure an adequate retirement income.

As the Commission pointed out, when faced with a pension gap, there are four options for society:

- Accept that pensioners will be poorer.
- Increase taxes or cut spending on other things in order to pay better pensions.
- Save extra.
- Retire later.

Setting aside the first option (poorer pensioners) and accepting that only governments can control the second (increasing taxes or cutting other spending), at a personal level you are left with just the last two options. If you personally face a **pension gap**, the ways to close it are to save more and/or retire later.

DO YOU HAVE A GAP?

It is very easy to underestimate the cost of retirement. Not every individual is saving too little, but the evidence suggests that the majority of people are.

The **calculator** on the opposite page will help you check whether you are on track for the retirement you want or whether you need to start saving extra. If you are a couple, each of you needs to fill it in separately.

> ### Jargon buster
>
> **Benefit statement** A statement issued by a pension scheme showing the amount of pension you might get at a specified age based on the amount of pension built up so far, the amount you might continue to build up if contributions are still being paid in, and various assumptions. See Chapters 4 to 7 for details.

Pension gap calculator

Find out if you have a pension gap by comparing Target retirement income (K) (page 22) with expected pensions income.

retirement, expressed in today's money. Add together these pensions and enter the total in box M.)

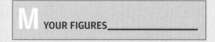

M YOUR FIGURES_____

YOUR TARGET RETIREMENT INCOME IN TODAY'S MONEY (£ A YEAR) (K)

(Result K1 or K2 from Retirement Income Calculator on page 22.)

K YOUR FIGURES_____

YOUR ANNUAL PENSION GAP IN TODAY'S MONEY (N)

(Subtract amounts L and M from K. If the result is zero or less, you are on track for your retirement income. If it is a positive number, you have a pension gap.)

N YOUR FIGURES_____

LESS EXPECTED STATE PENSION (L)

(From pension forecast or combined benefit statement – see Chapter 2. Usually expressed as a weekly amount. Multiply by 52 to get the annual equivalent and enter the result in box L.)

L YOUR FIGURES_____

LESS ANY PENSIONS YOU ARE ALREADY BUILDING UP (M)

(From benefit statements – see Chapters 4 to 7. Check the most recent benefit statement for each scheme for an estimate of what you can expect at

Case Study Gina

Gina is 50. After a break to bring up children, she returned to work and is now employed by a logistics firm. She will be relying partly on her husband for retirement income, but hopes to have her own income of about £11,000 a year when she retires. Gina benefited from home responsibilities protection (see page 41) and can expect to get the full state basic pension (£4,400 in 2006-7). Her state pension forecast also says she is on track for a state additional pension of £39.66 a week, which is just under £2,100 a year. Gina adds these together and enters £6,500 in box L.

She belongs to an occupational pension scheme and her latest benefit statement suggests her pension at age 65 might be £2,400 a year. Gina enters this amount in Box M.

Subtracting L and M from K leaves £2,100 a year. This is Gina's pension gap.

Saving via pension schemes

For many people the best way to plug a pension gap is to start saving (or save extra) through a pension scheme. The tax savings are considerable and there can be other powerful incentives.

Tax advantages

We have already looked briefly at the advantages that saving through a pension scheme has over other types of saving. These include:

- **Tax relief** on the contributions paid into the scheme.
- The resulting **pension fund** builds up largely tax-free.
- Part of the savings can be taken at retirement as a **tax-free lump sum** (though the rest must be drawn as taxable pension).

Using a pension scheme means you get tax relief while you save, but, apart from taking a tax-free lump sum on retirement, you are eventually taxed on the money you receive as pension income. You **defer tax** rather than save

it altogether. Whether you save tax in the long run depends on your top tax rate while you work compared with your tax rate when you retire.

The tables right assume that your invested pension fund grows at a rate of 6 per cent a year after deducting charges. How tax deferral treatment affects this rate of return depends on your tax rates while saving and while

Jargon buster

Contribution Money paid into a pension scheme by you or someone else, for example, your employer.

Pension fund A pool of investments into which contributions are paid and which is used to provide pensions and other pension scheme benefits as they fall due for payment.

Tax deferral Putting off a tax bill until a later time. This could save tax if your tax rate in future is lower than now.

> ❝ Tax incentives are a powerful reason to save for retirement through pension schemes. ❞

 To understand the pros and cons of different types of scheme see Chapters 4 and 5. Tax rates are an important consideration but there are other benefits and drawbacks you need to consider.

Effect of tax relief

The effect of pension scheme tax relief is shown below, assuming you can take the maximum possible tax-free sum. Blue figures indicate where you gain on balance from the tax treatment.

Your top tax rate when you pay into a scheme	Your top tax rate when your pension is paid			
	0.0%	10.0%	22.0%	40.0%
0% (non-taxpayer)	6.0%	5.2%	4.1%	2.3%
10% (starting rate)	7.1%	6.3%	5.2%	3.4%
22% (basic rate)	8.7%	7.8%	6.7%	4.9%
40% (higher rate)	11.6%	10.7%	9.6%	7.6%

Bonus from tax relief

The bonus gained when non-taxpayers and starting-rate taxpayers save through personal pensions is reflected in the figures below. Blue figures indicate where you gain on balance from the tax treatment.

Your top tax rate when you pay into a scheme	Your top tax rate when your pension is paid			
	0.0%	10.0%	22.0%	40.0%
0% (non-taxpayer)	8.7%	7.8%	6.7%	4.9%
10% (starting rate)	8.7%	7.8%	6.7%	4.9%
22% (basic rate)	8.7%	7.8%	6.7%	4.9%
40% (higher rate)	11.6%	10.7%	9.6%	7.6%

drawing your pension (assuming that you can take the maximum possible tax-free lump sum before starting your pension). Where tax deferral raises the rate of return above 6 per cent, you are saving tax overall which gives you an incentive to use a pension scheme. Where the rate of return is lower than 6 per cent, **tax deferral** has increased the tax you pay and you would probably be better off looking at other ways to save.

If you pay tax at a lower rate during retirement than you did while working, deferring tax boosts the effective return on your savings – not just because of the tax-free lump sum you can draw but also because the tax you pay on the pension is less than the tax relief you've had while your savings were building up.

If you pay tax at the same rate in retirement as you do while saving, there is still some incentive to use a pension scheme because of the tax-free lump sum.

If you are likely to pay a higher rate of tax in retirement than while saving, there is no incentive to use a pension scheme.

Guy is a self-employed photographer. He pays some money into a pension scheme when he can afford to. But his earnings are erratic, so he prefers to put a lot of his surplus - when business is going well - into other more flexible types of saving. That way he can draw the money out again when there's less work around.

You also might conclude that pension schemes offer a poor deal if you're a non-taxpayer while working, since the tax incentives appear irrelevant. But with some types of pension scheme, including **personal pensions** and **stakeholder pension schemes** (see Chapter 5), everyone is given tax relief at the **basic rate** (22 per cent in 2006-7) on the contributions they pay into pension schemes, regardless of their actual rate of tax. If you are a non-taxpayer or you pay tax at only the lowest rate (10 per cent), you still get tax relief at 22 per cent, which is effectively a bonus.

The second table on page 61 shows the effect of the tax treatment once this bonus is taken into account. The only people who do not have any tax incentive to save through pension schemes are the small minority who will pay tax at the higher-rate in retirement but pay tax at a lower rate now.

Other features of pension schemes

Tax incentives are a powerful reason to save for retirement through pension schemes. With **occupational pension schemes** (see Chapters 4 and 5), another very strong incentive is that your employer pays contributions into the scheme on your behalf – these are effectively an extra part of your pay package. Employers might also pay into your own personal pension (see Chapter 5) but their contributions, if any, might be low.

Running a pension scheme is a complex business requiring input from a variety of professionals, including actuaries, lawyers and fund managers. They all need to be paid and there are costs too in buying, selling and safely keeping the investments in the pension fund. The higher the charges, the less money left to provide pensions and other benefits. Occupational pension schemes usually have relatively low charges. But, with personal pensions and similar schemes that you take out on an individual basis, charges are often high.

The main drawback of saving through pension schemes is that they are inflexible. They are designed specifically to provide an income in later life. Usually you cannot get your money back early – whatever financial crisis you may be facing – and when you can get at your money most of it must be drawn in the form of a pension.

NON-PENSION SAVINGS AND INVESTMENTS

You can use any type of savings and investments as a way of saving for retirement. But, unless you are already very close to retiring, you will be saving over a long period. Historically, share-based investments have tended to produce much higher returns over long periods (say, ten years or more) than lower-risk investments, such as building society accounts (see Chapter 9 for more details). In most cases, if you save for retirement using **non-pension investments**, there are no particular tax incentives. An exception is if you invest through **individual savings accounts (ISAs)**.

Individual savings accounts

An ISA is not an investment as such. Think of it as a tax-free wrapper you can put around a whole range of different investments, including shares, unit trusts and savings accounts. There is no tax relief on money you pay in but the investments in the ISA grow either completely or largely tax free (depending on the type of investment) and there is no tax on money you draw out. There are no restrictions on when you can have your money back or in what form.

Each tax year until 2009-10, you have an **ISA allowance** of £7,000. You can either invest up to the full £7,000 in a 'maxi ISA' or you opt for

Your yearly ISA allowance

How you can allocate your annual ISA tax allowance

Your choice	Description	Maximum you can invest
Either one maxi ISA		
Maxi ISA	Must invest in stock-market investments such as shares and/or unit trusts. May also be partly invested in 'cash' (meaning a savings account or similar)	Up to £7,000 each tax year
Or one or both of the following mini ISA's		
Cash ISA	A bank, building society or National Savings & Investments savings account	Up to £3,000 each tax year
Stocks-and-shares mini ISA	Investing in stock-market investments, such as shares and unit trusts	Up to £4,000 each tax year

> **"Relying mainly or completely on selling property as a way of financing your retirement is a risky strategy."**

up to two 'mini ISAs'. A maxi ISA or a stocks-and-shares mini ISA could be suitable for long-term saving for retirement.

As a way to save for retirement, ISAs are more flexible than pension schemes since you can get your money back at any time and in any form you like.

Compared with using a pension scheme, ISAs are not quite as tax-efficient. Pension schemes give you tax relief as you pay your money in but tax it as you draw it out. ISAs are a mirror image: there's no tax relief on the way in but the proceeds are tax free. What gives pensions the edge is that you can usually take part of the proceeds as a tax-free lump sum – which means you get tax relief on both the way in and the way out.

Property

Since the 1970s UK house prices have – apart from an occasional blip – been on an upward trend with particularly steep rises since the mid-1990s. This has prompted a lot of interest in the potential for using residential property as a substitute for pension savings, either by buying a large home which can be traded down at retirement to release money for a pension or by investing in buy-to-let property.

Trading down to a smaller home at retirement is a tax-efficient strategy, since the gain made on selling your home is normally tax-free. Investing in buy-to-let property does not have this advantage, so any gain made when you sell would apart from various tax reliefs and allowances (for example, your annual tax-free allowance which was £8,800 in 2006-7) be taxable at up to a 40 per cent rate.

Relying mainly or completely on selling property as a way of financing retirement is a risky strategy. Who knows what the property market will be like in 30 or 40 years time? The government is keen to promote more house building which could take away a lot of the pressure on house prices. Even if house prices generally carry on rising, the particular properties that you own might not fare so well. A less risky alternative could be to invest in a **fund** that holds lots of different residential properties – see Chapter 9.

 Property funds offer a way of investing in a portfolio of many different properties and/or shares in property companies. This spreads your risk across a wider range. See page 182 for further information.

Different ways to save for retirement

You can save for your retirement in many ways, but with most non-pension investments there are no particular tax incentives, except in the case of ISAs. Flexibility is another issue you may want to consider.

Feature	Method of saving for retirement			
	Pension scheme	Individual savings account	Other non-pension investments	Direct investment in property
Your employer generally contributes	Yes, if occupational scheme. Sometimes in case of other schemes	No	No	No
Tax relief on money you pay in	Yes	No	No	No
Your investment builds up tax-free	Partly	Partly	Usually no	Yes, if the property is your home. Otherwise, no
Tax-free when you take your money out	No – you can often take part as a tax-free lump sum but the rest must be drawn as taxable pension	Yes	Usually no	Yes, if the property is your home. Otherwise, no
You can get your money back at any time	No, minimum age is 50 (rising to 55 by 2010)	Yes	Often – depends on the type of investment	Yes
You have flexibility over how much you cash in and when	No	Yes	Often – depends on the type of investment	When – yes, but must usually cash in whole property in one go

HOW MUCH SHOULD YOU SAVE?

If you have a **pension gap**, the key question is: how much (or how much extra) do you need to save to plug it? The tables opposite give some idea, assuming you opt to save through the sorts of pension schemes described in Chapter 5.

The tables show the amount you would need to save each month, after deducting tax relief at the basic rate, in order to produce £1,000 a year of pension (pre-tax) in today's money. You'll need to save less if your employer is willing to chip in. If you are a higher-rate taxpayer, the cost to you is less because you get extra tax relief – multiply the values from the tables by 0.77 to find the cost to you.

These tables show the how much you need to save each month, after deducting tax relief at the basic rate, to produce each £1000 a year of pension (pre-tax) in today's money.

The following assumptions have been made:

- Your monthly contributions increase in line with earnings assumed to increase by 4 per cent a year.

- Your contributions are net of tax relief at the basic rate.

- The pension fund investments grow by 6 per cent a year after charges have been deducted.

- At the chosen retirement age, the pension fund is converted into a pension which increases during retirement in line with price inflation. There are different tables for men and women because women's pensions are generally more expensive since they tend to live longer than men.

- The table for couples assumes the pension is taken out by a man for himself and a female partner and carries on paying out at two-thirds of its previous rate if the man dies first.

- All amounts are in today's money assuming inflation averages 2.5% a year between now and retirement.

Case Study Geoff

Geoff, aged 40, hopes to retire at age 65 with an income of £20,000 a year. Currently he's on target for only £15,000 so he has a £5,000 pension gap. The table to the right shows that he needs to start saving £39.61 a month for each extra £1,000 of income, so he needs to save 5 x £39.61 = £198 a month to plug the gap. If he puts off starting to save for just five years, the cost rises steeply to 5 x £55.95 = £280 a month.

Savings per month to produce each £1,000 a year of pension

Women

Your age now	\multicolumn{6}{c}{Your planned retirement age}
	50	55	60	65	70	75
20	£51.75	£34.49	£22.98	£14.94	£9.65	£6.39
25	£70.22	£45.54	£29.74	£19.04	£12.16	£7.98
30	£99.18	£61.79	£39.26	£24.64	£15.50	£10.05
35	£149.32	£87.28	£53.27	£32.53	£20.06	£12.81
40	£252.74	£131.40	£75.24	£44.14	£26.48	£16.58
45	£569.95	£222.41	£113.28	£62.34	£35.93	£21.89
50		£501.55	£191.73	£93.86	£50.74	£29.71
55			£432.37	£158.86	£76.40	£41.96
60				£358.25	£129.31	£63.18
65					£291.60	£106.93
70						£241.13

Men

Your age now	50	55	60	65	70	75
20	£47.44	£30.80	£20.19	£13.40	£8.30	£5.36
25	£64.37	£40.66	£26.13	£17.09	£10.45	£6.69
30	£90.92	£55.17	£34.50	£22.11	£13.33	£8.43
35	£136.88	£77.93	£46.81	£29.19	£17.25	£10.75
40	£231.67	£117.33	£66.12	£39.61	£22.77	£13.91
45	£522.45	£198.58	£99.55	£55.95	£30.90	£18.36
50		£447.8	£168.49	£84.23	£43.64	£24.92
55			£379.97	£142.57	£65.70	£35.19
60				£321.51	£111.20	£52.99
65					£250.78	£89.68
70						£202.24

Couples

Your age now	50/45	55/50	60/55	65/60	70/65	75/70
20	£54.21	£35.93	£24.68	£16.34	£11.21	£7.55
25	£73.56	£47.44	£31.94	£20.82	£14.13	£9.43
30	£103.90	£64.37	£42.17	£26.95	£18.01	£11.88
35	£156.43	£90.92	£57.22	£35.58	£23.31	£15.14
40	£264.77	£136.88	£80.81	£48.28	£30.77	£19.60
45	£597.09	£231.67	£121.67	£68.19	£41.75	£25.87
50		£522.45	£205.93	£102.66	£58.97	£35.11
55			£464.40	£173.76	£88.79	£49.59
60				£391.84	£150.28	£74.66
65					£338.89	£126.37
70						£284.97

WORKING LONGER

The tables on page 67 also illustrate why planning to work longer makes your pension more affordable. You can see that, as you move across each table to the right, each column corresponds to a later retirement age and the cost of each £1,000 of pension falls.

In 2006, new laws are due to start that outlaw age discrimination. From October 2006, your employer cannot make you retire earlier than age 65 unless there are objective reasons for doing so. Your employer will have to consider your request to work on beyond age 65 if you want to. If your employer does not follow the new rules, you will be able to claim unfair dismissal.

For more information, see the government website: www.dti.gov.uk/er/equality/age.htm.

The government has also changed the rules for occupational pension schemes (see Chapter 4) so that you are no longer forced to retire in order to start drawing a pension from your present employer's scheme. This opens the way for partial rather than full retirement. For example, you might – provided your employer and the pension scheme rules allow it – cut back your working hours and make up the consequent drop in pay

by starting to draw a small pension. Deferring the rest of your pension means it will be larger once it does start. Planning ahead to adopt this strategy means you can reduce the amount you need to save.

Ambitions like Natalie's (see case study above) to retire very early are looking increasingly unrealistic. As people live longer, retiring at 50 could mean spending as long or longer in retirement than working. Most people simply could not save enough while working to fund so many years of leisure.

Case Study Natalie

Natalie, aged 30, thinks it would be great to retire at 50 on a pension of, say, £15,000 a year. But, if she starts to save now, she needs to contribute 15 x £99.18 = £1,488 a month – that's nearly £18,000 a year and far more than Natalie can afford. By planning on a later retirement age of 65, she reduces the outlay to 15 x £24.64 = £591 a month (just over £7,000) which is still a lot but more manageable.

To check out how much pension a set level of monthly savings might produce at retirement, try the online calculator at www.pensioncalculator.org.uk (Association of British Insurers/Financial Services Authority).

Filling a pensions gap – your options

After calculating your pensions gap at the start of this chapter, here ia a quick overview of your options.

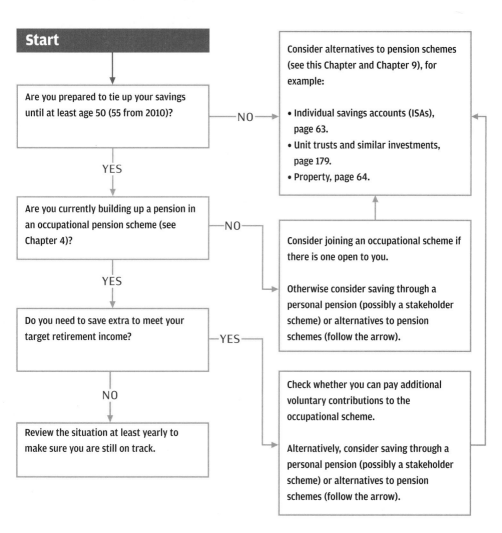

Start

Are you prepared to tie up your savings until at least age 50 (55 from 2010)?

— NO → Consider alternatives to pension schemes (see this Chapter and Chapter 9), for example:

- Individual savings accounts (ISAs), page 63.
- Unit trusts and similar investments, page 179.
- Property, page 64.

YES ↓

Are you currently building up a pension in an occupational pension scheme (see Chapter 4)?

— NO → Consider joining an occupational scheme if there is one open to you.

Otherwise consider saving through a personal pension (possibly a stakeholder scheme) or alternatives to pension schemes (follow the arrow).

YES ↓

Do you need to save extra to meet your target retirement income?

— YES → Check whether you can pay additional voluntary contributions to the occupational scheme.

Alternatively, consider saving through a personal pension (possibly a stakeholder scheme) or alternatives to pension schemes (follow the arrow).

NO ↓

Review the situation at least yearly to make sure you are still on track.

Limits to saving through pension schemes

There used to be restrictions on the amount you could pay into pension schemes. Since April 2006 ('A Day'), you have a lot more freedom which makes it much easier to plug even a large pension gap.

Annual contributions

There is no limit at all on how much you pay into pension schemes each year but you will get tax relief only on contributions paid before age 75 and up to this amount:

- A basic amount of £3,600, or
- If higher, an amount equal to your 'relevant earnings' for the tax year. This means your UK earnings on which you have paid income tax. They include wages, salaries and so on from a job plus the taxable value of any fringe benefits (such as a company car, medical insurance or cheap loans), profits from your business and/or income from property you let out on a commercial basis as furnished holiday accommodation. Relevant earnings do not include income from other property, savings, investments, pensions, state benefits and so on.

This is called your 'annual limit for relief'. It applies to the sum of your contributions to all your pension schemes.

Some types of contribution do not count towards the limit, for example, contributions paid by your employer, National Insurance rebates paid in because you are contracted out (see Chapter 6) and transfers you receive as part of a pension sharing arrangement on divorce (see Chapter 8). But otherwise contributions paid

❝ The generous limit on contributions that qualify for tax relief lets you pay large lump sums into a pension scheme. ❞

Jargon buster

Annual limit for relief The maximum contributions you can make to pension schemes each year which qualify for tax relief. The limit is £3,600 or, if higher, your total earnings for the year.

Case Study Arif

Arif has inherited £70,000 on the death of his mother. He would like to pay as much as possible of this into a pension scheme. His relevant earnings in 2006-7 are £40,000 on which he pays £7,734 income tax. If he pays £40,000 of the inheritance into a pension scheme, he will get tax relief on the full amount and the relief will come to £7,734 – in other words, he gets back all the income tax he paid on his earnings. There is no tax relief on any contributions over that amount, but he could make another large contribution next tax year.

in for you by someone else – for example, if your husband or wife makes payments into your scheme – do use up part of the limit.

The generous limit on contributions that qualify for tax relief lets you pay large lump sums into a pension scheme, for example, if you inherit money or have a sizeable lottery win.

Over the limit?

If you go over your **annual limit** for relief, any tax relief on the excess contributions must be paid back. The pension scheme will normally organise repaying any tax relief that was paid directly into the scheme. You

have to arrange repayment through your tax return of any relief that was given direct to you. The excess contributions can be left in the scheme or repaid to you. Any repayment must be made within six years of the end of the tax year in which the excess payment occurred.

Your annual allowance

You have an **annual allowance** each year which sets the amount by which your total pension savings can increase. In any tax year when your savings increase by more you have to pay tax on the excess at a rate of 40 per cent.

For 2006-7 the annual limit is £215,000. In 2007-8 it will go up to £225,000, in 2008-9 £235,000, 2009-10 £245,000 and 2010-11 £255,000. The government has said that future increases in the annual limit will reflect economic factors such as price inflation.

The annual allowance applies to the increase in value of all your savings through pension schemes. How you measure the increase in value depends on the type of scheme:

● **Defined benefit scheme** (see Chapter 4). Each year you usually see an increase in the amount of pension you are promised at

To find out more on pension limits and the impact of 'A Day' changes generally, consult The Pensions Advisory Service (TPAS) website on www.pensionsadvisoryservice.org.uk or call their national helpline on 0845 601 2923.

retirement. To convert this into a value that can be compared with the annual limit, the pension is multiplied by a factor of 10. For example, if your promised pension goes up by £1,000 a year, this is treated as an increase in your pension savings of 10 x £1,000 = £10,000. You also take into account any increase in a tax-free lump sum payable automatically at retirement.

- **Money purchase scheme** (see Chapter 5). The increase in value is the sum of contributions paid into the scheme by you, on your behalf and, if applicable, by your employer.
- **Cash balance scheme** (see Chapter 4). The increase in value is the change in the amount of pension fund you are promised at retirement, but you ignore any increase in line with inflation up to a maximum of 5 per cent.

The yearly growth in most people's pension savings will be much less than their annual allowance. Only a small proportion of the population are likely to have to worry about exceeding this allowance. If that applies to you, consult an independent financial adviser or pensions adviser.

Your lifetime allowance

Your **lifetime allowance** is a value of benefits (pensions, tax-free lump sums and payments to your survivors if you die) that can be drawn from all of your pension schemes without a special tax charge being payable.

❝Contributions paid in for you by someone else – for example, if your husband or wife makes payments into your scheme – do use up part of the limit.❞

Each time a pension or other benefit is drawn from one of your pension schemes, the value of the benefit uses up part of your lifetime allowance. If the value of the latest benefit being drawn exceeds the remaining allowance, you are charged tax on the excess. Tax is levied at 55

Jargon buster

Defined benefit scheme Type of pension scheme that promises you a set level of pension typically based on your pay and length of time in the scheme.

Money purchase scheme Type of pension scheme where the pension you get depends on the amount paid in, how well the invested contributions grow and the amount of pension you can buy at retirement with the resulting fund.

Cash balance scheme Type of pension scheme that promises you a set amount of pension fund at retirement for each year you have been in the scheme. The pension you get then depends on how much pension you can buy with fund.

per cent of the excess if you draw it as a lump sum or 25 per cent if you leave the excess in the scheme and draw it as taxable pension.

The standard lifetime allowance for 2006-7 is £1.5 million. For 2007-8 this will increase to £1.6 million, 2008-9 £1.65 million, 2009-10 £1.75 million and 2010-11 £1.8 million. The government has said that future increases in the lifetime limit will reflect economic factors such as price inflation.

In some circumstances (see below) your lifetime allowance may be higher than the standard amount.

To compare benefits against the lifetime allowance, you work out the value of the benefits broadly as follows:

- **Tax-free lump sum at retirement.** The amount you get.
- **Pension from defined benefit scheme.** The pension multiplied by a factor of 20. For example a pension of £8,000 a year would use up 20 x £8,000 = £160,000 of your lifetime allowance.
- **Pension from other types of scheme.** The amount of pension fund being used or set aside to provide the pension.
- **Lump sum paid to your heirs if you die before aged 75.** The amount they get.

The value of most people's pensions and other benefits is well below the level of the lifetime allowance. Only

about 1 per cent of the population is likely to go over the allowance and so have to pay tax. If this could apply, get help from an independent financial adviser or other pensions adviser.

EXISTING LARGE PENSION SAVINGS

There are special rules to help people who might otherwise have lost out when the new tax rules for pensions started in April 2006. In general, they are relevant only for people who had built up large pension savings.

❝The value of most people's pensions and other benefits is well below the level of the lifetime allowance.❞

Primary protection

If the value of your pension savings and rights already exceeded the standard lifetime allowance (£1.5 million) at 5 April 2006, you can register for protection so you do not have to pay tax on the excess. This is called 'primary protection'.

Primary protection works by giving you your own lifetime allowance which is higher than the standard amount. For example, if the value of your pension savings and rights stood at £1.9 million on 5 April 2006, that would be your lifetime allowance.

You can carry on building up further pension savings but these will create an excess over and above your personal lifetime allowance and so trigger a tax charge when benefits are taken. Similarly if your existing savings grow faster than the increases in the lifetime allowance, you would build up an excess which would be taxable.

Enhanced protection

You can register to have the pension savings and rights you had built up by 5 April 2006 fully protected from any tax charge. This is called '**enhanced protection**' and is available whether or not the value of your savings exceeded the standard lifetime allowance at 5 April 2006.

With enhanced protection, even if your existing pension savings grew faster than increases in the lifetime allowance, there would be no tax charge on the excess. But you are not allowed to make any new pension savings after 5 April 2006. If you do, the enhanced protection is automatically lost – though you could switch to primary protection.

Work-related pension schemes

Work-related pension schemes are available to employees. The most common characteristic is that contributions are deducted directly from your pay and passed to the scheme provider. Your employer normally also pays into the scheme on your behalf, providing a significant boost to your pension savings.

If you are an employee, you will normally be able to join a pension scheme through your workplace. There are three main types of scheme that might be on offer:

- **Occupational scheme.** This is organised by your employer who pays into the scheme on your behalf, though you are usually required to contribute too. Membership is offered as part of your overall pay package. When you leave your employer, you stop being an active member of the scheme. The two main types are final salary schemes (see page 82) and money purchase schemes (see page 88).
- **Group personal pension scheme (GPP).** This is a personal pension (see Chapter 5) run by an insurance company. Your employer does not have to pay anything towards the scheme, but might agree to do so.

￼Membership of a good occupational scheme is a valuable part of your overall pay package. ￼

Your employer might have negotiated with the insurance company for some favourable terms for members, for example, low charges. The scheme is personal to you so, when you leave your employer, you can carry on paying into the scheme if you want to.

- **Stakeholder pension scheme.** This is also a personal pension but has some special features, such as a cap on charges and flexible contributions (see Chapter 5). If your employer has five or more employees and does not offer either an occupational scheme or a GPP to which the employer contributes at least 3 per cent of your pay, there must be a workplace stakeholder scheme. Your employer does not have to pay anything into your stakeholder scheme, but might agree to do so. When you leave your employer, you can carry on paying into the scheme if you want to.

With all these **workplace schemes**, there is usually an arrangement for your own contributions to be deducted direct from your pay and passed automatically to the scheme provider.

There is no essential difference between a GPP or workplace stakeholder scheme and the types of personal pension and stakeholder scheme that you arrange for yourself, so turn to Chapter 5 to find out more about these. This chapter looks at **occupational pension schemes**.

Occupational schemes

These offer a pension organised by your employer, who pays into the scheme on your behalf, though you are usually required to contribute too. They are usually hard to beat as a way of saving for retirement.

Employers are not obliged to offer occupational pension schemes. Many do as a way of attracting and retaining staff. You do not have to join, but membership of a good scheme is a valuable part of your pay package.

Tax advantages

Like all pension schemes, occupational ones have tax advantages (see Chapter 3). However, you do not get any tax relief on contributions you pay into an occupational scheme unless you are a taxpayer, since whatever you pay into the scheme is deducted direct from your pay before income tax is worked out. Unlike the schemes described in Chapter 5, there is no mechanism for giving a bonus to non-taxpayers and starting-rate taxpayers (see page 106).

Benefits

The table on page 78 summarises what a good occupational scheme typically offers. Your employer usually pays a substantial part of the cost of

these benefits and often separately meets the bill for running the scheme. These advantages make an occupational scheme hard to beat as a way of saving for retirement. Just over half of all full-time employees belong to occupational schemes.

Although there has been a lot of news coverage about occupational schemes closing 'in deficit' with members losing some or even all of their pensions, keep this in

Case Study | Hank

Hank earns £30,000 a year and is a basic rate taxpayer. In 2006-7, his tax bill would normally be £5,234. But Hank pays 5 per cent of his salary into the pension scheme (5% x £30,000 = £1,500 for the year). This reduces his tax bill to £4,904. This means Hank has had tax relief of £5,234 - £4,904 = £330. The tax relief comes to 22 per cent of £1,500, in other words.

 For information about specific details of your occupational pension scheme, contact the pension scheme administrator, who is usually located in the personnel department in a company or workplace.

Benefits from a typical occupational pension scheme

Type of benefit	Description
Retirement benefits	From normal pension age: • Pension • Tax-free lump sum
Early retirement benefits	Reduced pension if you choose to retire early
Ill-health benefits	Pension if you have to retire early due to illness or disability
Death benefits	• Pension for your spouse/civil partner (and in some schemes other partners) if you die before or after retirement • Pension for children/other dependants if you die • Lump sum payable to anyone you nominate if you die before the age of 75 (scheme rules may specify earlier age)

perspective. Around 0.5 per cent of occupational scheme members have been affected. The risk of poverty in old age through failing to save is greater than the risk of loss through joining an occupational scheme. See Chapter 10 for more information.

Restrictions/discrimination

An occupational scheme may be open to all employees or restricted to a particular group – for example, one scheme for works staff, another for management. A scheme is not allowed to discriminate on the basis of sex, sexual orientation, disability or religion.

Chapter 3 looked briefly at the effect new age discrimination laws will have on retirement ages from October 2006. (Your employer will not normally be able to retire you before age 65 and must consider your request to work on longer if you want to.) The legislation also applies to occupational pension schemes but will have little practical effect since most of the age-related rules that are part of occupational schemes' design are exempted. For example, occupational schemes will continue to be able to set a normal pension age from which your full pension is payable and to specify minimum and maximum ages at which you are eligible to join a scheme.

In general, pension schemes may not treat part-time workers less favourably than their full-time counterparts. This includes giving equal access to the scheme.

Jargon buster

Civil partner Since 5 December 2005, same-sex couples have been able to register their relationship as a civil partnership and, for most purposes, are then treated in the same way as husbands and wives.

DIFFERENT TYPES OF OCCUPATIONAL PENSION SCHEME

There are two fundamental types of occupational pension scheme and some important variations – see the table below.

SALARY-RELATED SCHEMES: THE PENSION PROMISE

Salary-related schemes are unlike most other types of saving and investment. You are promised (but not guaranteed) a certain level of pension in relation to your earnings regardless of the amount you pay in. This means you can plan ahead with some certainty because you know roughly how much pension to expect as a proportion of your current earnings.

In a contributory scheme, you'll be required to pay something towards the cost of meeting the pension promise and your employer pays the balance. In a non-contributory scheme, you

Main types of occupational pension scheme

Scheme	Description	Where to find more information
Salary-related (also called 'defined benefit')	The pension you get is worked out according to a formula based on your pay and length of time in the scheme	This chapter – see pages 79-81
Final salary	The most common type of salary-related schemes	See page 82
Career average	A type of salary-related scheme	See page 87
Money purchase (also called 'defined contribution')	Your pension depends on how much is paid into the scheme, how well the invested contributions grow and how much pension you can get for your pension fund at retirement	Pages 88-9 give a brief introduction; for further information, see Chapter 5
Cash balance	A type of money purchase scheme	See page 92
Hybrid	Combines elements of both salary-related and money purchase schemes	See page 92

> **"The risk of poverty in old age through failing to save is greater than the risk of loss through joining an occupational scheme."**

pay nothing and your employer meets the full cost.

Most private sector schemes are funded, which means the contributions paid in are invested to build up a fund from which the promised pensions are paid. Whatever you contribute is usually a fixed percentage of your pay – say 5 or 6 per cent. The amount your employer has to pay varies depending in particular on:

- How well the invested contributions grow. If investment performance is good, the cost to your employer is less. If investment performance is poor, your employer has to pay more.
- The cost of the pensions once they start to be paid. The major factor here is how long the pensioners live on average. The total cost of a pension for someone who lives many years will be greater than the cost for someone who dies soon after retirement. If – as currently – average life expectancy is rising, the cost of the pension scheme to the employer rises.

In this way, with a **salary-related scheme**, your employer rather than you bears most of the risk involved in saving for retirement.

The main risk you bear is that your employer can't afford to keep the pension promise – but see Chapter 10 for how you may be protected. This risk is low if you are in a public sector scheme where, in most cases, there is no pension fund. Instead, current contributions pay current pensions with any shortfall made up out of general tax revenues. Since, in the last resort, the government could raise taxes, there is little risk of public sector schemes failing to deliver the promised pensions already built up.

Jargon buster

Contributory scheme Pension scheme to which you are required to pay contributions.

Non-contributory scheme Pension scheme where you pay no contributions and your employer bears the full cost of the scheme.

Life expectancy The number of years a person of a specified age is expected to live.

 To find out more on pension limits and the impact of 'A Day' changes generally, consult The Pensions Advisory Service (TPAS) website on www.pensionsadvisoryservice.org.uk or call their national helpline on 0845 601 2923.

SALARY-RELATED OCCUPATIONAL PENSION SCHEMES

If your workplace offers this type of scheme, you are almost certain to benefit from joining it. The pros and cons listed below show why this is the case.

Salary-related occupational pension schemes normally offer considerable benefits to their members. Traditional-style 'final salary' schemes (based on your pay shortly before retirement) are particularly advantageous, with a promised pension which is partly protected against inflation. 'Career average' schemes (based on average pay over your whole career) offer similar benefits but are less expensive for employers and pay out less to those whose earnings peak in later life.

Pros

- Tax advantages (as for all private pension schemes)

- Predictable pension benefits

- Some protection against inflation

- Employer pays some or all of the costs of providing pensions and other benefits

- Employer might separately pay running costs

- Employer not you bears risks of poor investment performance and rising life expectancy

Cons

- Can be difficult to understand

- You might lose out when changing jobs (see Chapter 7)

- Scheme might close if your employer finds it too costly or risky (see Chapter 10)

- In worst case scenario, scheme might close without being able to pay the promised pensions (see Chapter 10)

Final salary schemes

Final salary schemes are currently the most commonly used type of salary-related scheme. Most public sector schemes are final salary. Big employers in the private sector have also tended to favour them. However, because of their high cost, these schemes may become less popular in future.

Final salary schemes are occupational schemes which offer a pension worked out as a proportion of your pay at or near retirement (or when you leave the scheme if earlier – see Chapter 7).

A big advantage of final salary schemes is that your **promised pension** is automatically protected against inflation while it is building up because the promised pension rises as your earnings increase.

How much pension?

Different schemes work out the promised pension in different ways, but typically you might get 1/60th, 1/80th or 1/100th of your final salary for each year you have been in the scheme. The fraction you get is called the 'accrual rate'. For example, if your final salary is £24,000 and you have been in a 1/60th scheme for 30 years your pension would be 30 x 1/60 x £24,000 = £12,000 a year. The general formula for working out your pension is:

Years in scheme x Accrual rate x Final salary = Pension

The table left shows how, for each £1,000 of final salary, your pension would build up in a final salary scheme. Usually the maximum pension you are allowed is 40 years' worth – for example 40/60th (a pension equal to two-thirds of your final salary) or 40/80th (half your final salary).

For pensions which start to be paid on or after 6 April 2005, salary-related schemes are required by law to increase pensions in line with price inflation up to a maximum of 2.5 per

How pension builds up in a final salary scheme

Number or years in the scheme	Pension built up for each £1,000 of your final salary if accrual rate is:		
	1/60th	1/80th	1/100th
1	£16.67	£12.50	£10.00
5	£83.33	£62.50	£50.00
10	£166.67	£125.00	£100.00
15	£250.00	£187.50	£150.00
20	£333.33	£250.00	£200.00
25	£416.67	£312.50	£250.00
30	£500.00	£375.00	£300.00
35	£583.33	£437.50	£350.00
40	£666.67	£500.00	£400.00

Case Study Dziko

Dziko expects to clock up 25 years' membership of her employer's final salary scheme by the time she retires. It is a 1/80th scheme. Based on her present final salary of £36,000 a year, she can expect a pension at retirement of 25 x 1/80 x £36,000 = £11,250 a year.

Alternatively, she could work out the expected pension using the table on page 82: the figure corresponding to 25 and 1/80th is £312.50; multiplying this by 36 gives £11,250.

cent a year. Schemes can choose to make bigger increases.

What is your final salary?

Final salary is defined in the rules of your scheme. It can have a variety of meanings: for example, average pay over the last three years, the average over a three year period ending within the last ten, or your annual earnings on a specified date. Check what definition your scheme uses.

Only your **'pensionable earnings'** are included in the calculation. This might be just your basic salary. A more generous definition would also include overtime pay, bonuses, commission and/or other payments. Some schemes reduce pensionable earnings to take account of the basic pension you will get from the state.

Pensionable earnings are also normally used as the basis for setting the contributions you pay if you are in a contributory scheme.

Tax-free lump sum

Most final salary schemes let you take a **tax-free lump sum** when you start your pension. You can use this money in any way you like – buy a new car, take a holiday, home improvements, boost your savings, and so on. It can be tempting to take as much tax-free cash as possible but this may be a poor deal.

The tax rules limit the maximum tax-free lump sum you can have. Your scheme's own rules might limit you to a smaller lump sum but, under the tax

Jargon buster

Accrual rate In a salary-related pension scheme, the proportion of your pay that you get as pension for each year you have been in the scheme.

Pensionable earnings The definition of pay used by a salary-related scheme when working out the pension it will pay and for setting contributions.

For advice on what to look out for – and what to do – if your scheme appears to be at risk (see Chapter 10).

rules, the maximum lump sum you can take at retirement is broadly the lower of

either:

- A quarter of the value of the benefits you are drawing, calculated by adding together the lump sum and the value of the pension. To work out the value of the pension, multiply the annual amount by a factor of 20. For example, if the remaining pension is £12,000, its value is 20 x £12,000 = £240,000 and the maximum lump sum would be £80,000 since this is a quarter of £240,000 + £80,000 = £320,000

or

- A quarter of the standard lifetime allowance (see page 72) remaining after deducting the value of any pension and other benefits you have taken so far.

The tax rules require that you take any lump sum before reaching age 75 and within three months of becoming entitled to your pension.

The commutation factor

In a 1/80th or 1/100th scheme, typically the lump sum will be in addition to your pension worked out as above. In a 1/60th scheme, the scheme rules normally require you to give up part of your pension if you want to have a tax-free lump sum – this is called 'commutation'.

The scheme sets a 'commutation factor' which says how much lump sum you get for each £1 of pension you give up. A common factor is 12 so, for example, if you gave up £1,000 a year of pension, you would get a tax-free lump sum of £12,000. Many schemes offer a higher commutation factor to women than men reflecting the higher cost of pensions for women since they tend to live longer.

It can be tempting to take the largest lump sum possible at

Case Study Colin

Colin has been a member of a 1/60th scheme for 20 years. He is about to start his pension and his final salary is £27,000. He has the option of taking a pension of 20 x 1/60 x £27,000 = £9,000 a year or taking a tax-free lump sum plus a lower pension.

The scheme rules let him swap £1 of pension for each £12 of lump sum. He reckons he could manage with £7,500 pension which would let him take a lump sum of 1,500 x £12 = £18,000. This is well within the limits allowed by the tax rules.

If Colin had to use the £18,000 to buy on the open market a pension that increased in line with inflation, in late 2005 he would have got only about £840 a year pension – much less than the £1,500 pension he has given up to get the lump sum. This means the commutation factor offered by the scheme is a poor deal.

Most schemes set their own normal pension age from which your full pension is payable and typically this is 65 at present. Although schemes are allowed to set a lower normal pension age, from October 2006 onwards it will be illegal for employers to set a normal retirement age below 65 (see page 78).

retirement since it is tax-free and you can use it in any way that you like. In the past, you were often advised to take a lump sum even if you needed the pension because you could invest the cash tax efficiently to produce income. But, over the last 15 years, it has become clear that people generally are living longer which is making pensions more expensive. Commutation factors have not kept up with the increase and are now often poor value. For example, to get good value, someone aged 65 should expect to be offered a lump sum of over £20 for each £1 of pension given up.

Starting your pension

As with all pension schemes, the tax rules say that your pension must normally start between age 50 (rising to 55 by 6 April 2010) and 75. Provided your employer and the schemes rules allow it, you do not have to retire to start a pension from your employer's scheme. And there is nothing to stop you taking work elsewhere after starting to draw a pension.

Retiring early

If you choose to retire earlier than the normal pension age for your scheme, your pension will usually be a lot lower because:

- It will be based on fewer years of membership.
- Once it starts, the pension will at best generally increase only in line with prices whereas while it is still

Case Study Rick

So far Rick has been a member of his 1/80th pension scheme for 26 years. Based on his current salary of £38,000, Rick (now aged 56) can expect a pension at the normal pension age of 65 equal to 35 x 1/80 x £ 38,000 = £16,625 a year. But he would like to retire early at age 60. This means his pension would be based on 30 years' membership. His scheme also makes an actuarial reduction of 6 per cent for each year of early retirement. So his pension from age 60 would be 70% x (30 x 1/80 x £38,000) = £9,975 a year. Retiring just five years early would reduce his pension by 40 per cent.

building up it is increasing in line with your earnings (which tend to increase by more than prices).

- The scheme will usually impose an 'actuarial reduction' to reflect the extra cost of paying your pension over a longer period. A common reduction is 6 per cent for each year below normal pension age.

If your employer is looking for voluntary redundancies, you might be offered a better-than-normal early retirement package – for example, the actuarial reduction might be waived.

Case Study Holly

The normal pension age for Holly's scheme is 65 but her employer agrees to her carrying on working for another five years. At age 65, she would have qualified for a pension of 31/60th of her final salary. But the scheme lets her continue building up pension at the normal rate, so by age 70 she gets 36/60th of her final salary. As her final salary is then £42,000, she retires on a pension of 36 x 1/60 x £42,000 = £25,200 a year.

Salary-related schemes often pay higher pensions if you have to retire early because of ill health. For example, there might be no actuarial reduction and the pension might be based on the number of years' membership you would have had if you had been able to work on until the normal pension age. Under the tax rules, your pension can start earlier than 50 (55) if you have to retire early because of ill health.

Retiring later

If you put off drawing your pension beyond the normal pension age for your scheme, you may be entitled to a larger pension once it does start. For example, in a 1/60th scheme, you might be allowed to carry on building up pension at a rate of 1/60th of final salary for each extra year of membership perhaps up to a maximum of, say 45/60th. Alternatively, the pension you had built up by normal pension age might be increased, say, in line with price inflation up to the point at which it starts. Check the rules for your particular scheme.

Career average schemes

A career average scheme is very similar to a final salary scheme but, instead of your pension being based on your pay at or near retirement, it is based on the average of your pensionable earnings over all the years you have been a member of the scheme.

The government has indicated that to cut the cost of providing pensions for public sector employees, it would like to switch to **career average** schemes in place of some final salary schemes. Also, some big private sector employers plan to switch from final salary to career average schemes.

How much pension?

As with a final salary scheme, your pension is worked out according to a formula:

Years in scheme x Accrual rate x Average salary = Pension

And the accrual rate will typically be 1/60th or 1/80th. Because salaries tend to rise over time as a result of inflation, usually earnings from earlier years are revalued to put them into today's money before your average salary figure is worked out.

If you are the sort of employee whose earnings tend to peak in later life as your career progresses, a career average scheme will give you a lower pension than you would have had from a final salary scheme.

Case Study Jacinda

Jacinda has been in a career average scheme for the last ten years. The table below shows her pensionable earnings over those years and how her career average salary is worked out from them. It is a 1/80th scheme, so based on her membership so far, she has built up a promised pension of 10 x 1/80 x £26,570 = £3,321 a year.

How Jacinda's salary is worked out

Year	Pensionable earnings (A)	Increase in national average earnings up to 2005-6 (B)	Pension earnings revalued to 2005-6 money Ax (1+B)
1996-7	£16,000	47.70%	£23,632
1997-8	£17,300	40.70%	£24,341
1998-9	£17,500	34.50%	£23,538
1999-2000	£18,500	29.10%	£23,884
2000-1	£22,000	21.40%	£26,708
2001-2	£23,000	16.80%	£26,864
2002-3	£25,000	11.90%	£27,975
2003-4	£25,500	8.10%	£27,566
2004-5	£29,000	4.10%	£30,189
2005-6	£31,000	n/a	£31,000
Average			£26,570

Money purchase schemes

The main alternative to salary-related schemes. The pension you get depends on how much is invested and how well the investments perform. They are easy to understand but offer no pension promise, making planning ahead for retirement unpredictable and risky.

'Money purchase' describes any pension scheme where the amount of pension you get at retirement depends on:

- The amount paid into the scheme.
- How well the invested contributions grow.
- The charges deducted.
- 'Annuity rates' which determine how much pension you get from the fund that has built up.

Jargon buster

Annuity An investment where you swap a lump sum (such as a pension fund) for an income either for life or a specified number of years. You cannot get your money back as a lump sum.
Annuity rate The amount of pension you get in return for your lump sum.

Many occupational schemes are money purchase schemes. So too are most other types of pension scheme, including personal pensions and stakeholder schemes. This chapter looks at features specific to **occupational money purchase schemes**. For aspects common to all money purchase schemes, see Chapter 5.

Unlike salary-related schemes, with a money purchase scheme, your employer simply pays in a set amount in contributions. This means the employer knows just how much it will cost to provide the scheme and bears no risk of costs running out of control. If investment returns are poor or pensions become more expensive because people are living longer, you get less pension rather than your employer having to pay more. For these reasons, many employers are turning away from final salary schemes and offering employees

 Transferring to or from a money purchase scheme is more straightforward than a salary-related scheme. See Chapter 7, page 143-147 for details.

Pros and cons of occupational money purchase schemes

Pros	Cons
Tax advantages (as with any private pension scheme)	Unpredictable amount of pension and other benefits – in other words, you bear all the risks
Employer pays some or all of the cost	Employer tends to pay less of the cost than with a salary-related scheme
Employer sometimes pays running costs separately	No automatic protection against inflation
Simple to understand	
Easy to transfer if you change jobs (see Chapter 7)	

money purchase schemes instead – see Chapter 10.

The table above summarises the main advantages and drawbacks of occupational money purchase schemes

How much pension

You can't know in advance how much pension you'll get from a money purchase scheme. But, with an occupational scheme, there are some features that help towards a good pension:

- **Amount paid in.** Your employer contributes on your behalf. Generally employer contributions are nowhere near as high as the amounts employers pay into salary-related schemes – see table on page 90 –

but they still provide a significant boost to your pension savings.

- **Charges.** Occupational schemes are often large and can negotiate lower charges than you would pay if arranging your own money purchase scheme.
- **Annuity rates.** Again because of their size, occupational schemes can often negotiate better annuity rates than you can get yourself. However, when you come to draw the pension you do not have to take the annuity offered by the scheme - you have the option instead to shop around for your own (see Chapter 5).

Unlike salary-related schemes, for pensions started from 6 April 2005 onwards, there is no requirement for

Private sector occupational schemes

Generally, employer contributions to money purchase schemes are not as high as those paid into salary-related schemes, although they still provide a significant boost to employees' pension savings.

Types of scheme	Average employer contribution	Average employee contributions [1]
Salary-related scheme	12.1%	4.6%
Money purchase scheme	6.2%	2.9%

1 Includes non-contributory schemes (where employee contributions are 0%).

the pension from a money purchase occupational scheme to be increased each year in line with inflation. It is left to you to decide whether you want an inflation-linked pension – see Chapter 5 for guidance on making this choice.

Tax-free lump sum

When you become entitled to start your pension, the tax rules let you take up a tax-free lump sum up to the lower of:

• A quarter of the fund that has built up, and

Case Study Geoff

Geoff has built up a pension fund of £28,000 and the scheme rules let him take up to a quarter of this as a tax-free lump sum. If he starts his pension now, he could have 25% x £28,000 = £7,000.

• A quarter of the standard lifetime allowance (see page 72) less the value of any benefits you have already taken.

The scheme might set its own lower limits.

Unlike a salary-related scheme, there are no commutation factors determining how much pension you give up in order to take a tax-free lump sum. The amount of pension you give up depends directly on the annuity rate at which the pension would have been bought. This is considered in detail in Chapter 5 but, generally, even if you need as much income as possible, it is worth taking the maximum tax-free lump sum. If need be, you can then invest the lump sum tax-efficiently to produce an income.

Starting your pension

The rules are the same as for final salary schemes. Your pension must start between age 50 (55 from 6 April 2010) and 75. You do not necessarily have to retire to start drawing pension from your employer's scheme- and there is nothing to stop you from taking work elsewhere after starting to draw a pension (see page 85).

Retiring early

If you retire earlier than the normal pension age, your pension will be lower because:

- You will miss out on the contributions which would have been paid in if you had put off drawing your pension until later.
- You reduce the time the pension fund is invested so miss out on some of the growth you might have had.
- The pension fund will buy less pension per year reflecting the fact that it has to be paid out for longer.

Some employers separately offer 'group income protection insurance' to pay out an income up to normal pension age if you have to retire early because of ill health.

Retiring later

If you retire later than the normal pension age for your scheme, you may get a larger pension when it does start because:

- The pension fund continues to be invested and so hopefully will carry on growing – see Chapter 9 for guidance on how to invest in this situation.
- Extra contributions may be paid in. Check to see if your employer will carry on making contributions beyond normal pension age.

Case Study Palab

Palab, 60, has been in a money purchase scheme for 30 years. He pays in 5 per cent of his earnings (currently £30,000 a year) and his employer adds a further 6 per cent. He had intended to work on until age 65 but is considering retiring now instead. By 65, his pension fund might buy an inflation-linked pension of £8,100 a year. If he retires now, he will lose five years' pension fund growth, miss out on 5 x (5% + 6%) x £30,000 = £16,500 of contributions and get a lower annuity rate because the pension has to be paid for longer. These factors reduce his pension by more than a third to £5,200 a year.

Planning point

In a money purchase scheme, it is usually worth taking the largest possible tax-free lump sum.

CASH BALANCE SCHEMES

Cash balance schemes are a type of money purchase scheme that spreads the risks more evenly between you and your employer. In a normal money purchase scheme, your employer pays a set contribution to the scheme on your behalf and leaves you to run the risk of how well or poorly the invested contributions grow. In a **cash balance scheme**, your employer promises you a set amount of pension fund at retirement for each year you are in the scheme and pays in however much is needed to keep that promise. So your employer – not you – bears the investment risk while your pension fund is building up. You still bear the risk of a low pension if the cost of pensions rises as people live longer.

HYBRID SCHEMES

Hybrid schemes combine salary-related and money purchase elements to reduce the risks you bear by giving you a limited pension promise. They work in a variety of ways. For example, in a final salary underpin scheme, you are promised a pension at least equal to an amount worked out on a final salary basis. But the contributions are invested and, if the pension fund would buy a bigger pension than the salary-related one, you get the money purchase pension instead.

TRIVIAL PENSIONS

If the value of your pension savings and pension rights in all the schemes you have (occupational, personal and so on) comes to no more than 1 per cent of the **standard lifetime allowance** (in other words 1% x £1.5 million = £15,000 in 2006-7), the tax rules let you take the whole lot as a lump sum.

You must be under age 75 and the rules of each pension scheme concerned must allow the commutation of trivial pensions.

Only a quarter of the lump sum will be tax-free. The rest is taxed as if it were pension income received in the tax year the lump sum is paid. The amount of tax you pay depends on your allowances and other income for that year.

Increasing your pension

If you are on track for a low pension from your occupational scheme, you have several options to improve the situation. These include making additional voluntary contributions (AVCs), and possibly joining an employer's salary sacrifice scheme.

The three main ways of boosting your occupational pension are to:

- Pay extra contributions (see below).
- Start your pension later (see pages 86 and 91).
- Consider salary sacrifice if available (see page 96).

Extra contributions

Many employers run in-house 'additional voluntary contribution (AVC)' schemes which let you pay in extra to build up extra benefits. They work in one of two ways:

- **Added years scheme.** This is available only with salary-related schemes and found mainly in the public sector (for example, in schemes covering teachers and NHS workers). Your AVCs buy extra years, so that when the formula is used to work out your pension (and other benefits) the amount is higher.
- **Money purchase AVCs.** This is available with any type of occupational scheme. Your AVCs are invested and build up a fund. This can be used to provide extra

pension, buy other benefits such as life cover (see Chapter 8) or increase your tax-free lump sum.

Extra contributions using added years schemes

As discussed above, in a final salary scheme or career average scheme, your pension is worked out according to a formula:

Years in scheme x Accrual rate x Your pay = Pension

An added years scheme lets you buy extra years so that the 'years in scheme' part of the formula is higher

Planning point

If you are in a salary-related scheme, especially a public sector one, check with your pension scheme administrator whether you can buy added years and, if so, on what terms. Many public sector schemes have websites where you can check the rules and use online calculators to work out what you'd have to pay.

93

than the actual number of years for which you have been a scheme member. In most schemes, there is a maximum number of years that you can have in total – say, 40 or 45 – so there is a cap on the overall pension you can build up this way.

Whether buying added years is good value depends crucially on how much you are charged for each year. Generally, the closer you are to normal pension age and/or the higher your salary, the more expensive the added years will be.

Often you will have a choice of either paying for the added years through an increase in your regular contributions to the scheme over a selected time period or in a single lump sum. You may even be able to use the tax-free lump sum you get at the point at which you start your pension to buy added years at the last minute.

Extra contributions using an in-house money purchase scheme

In-house money purchase AVC schemes are essentially no different from any other money purchase scheme and Chapter 5 describes in detail how these work. But there are some special features of an in-house AVC scheme that you should consider:

- **Charges and investment choice.** Typically the scheme will be run for your employer by an insurance company or, sometimes, a building society. Your employer may have been able to negotiate a good deal so that the charges are lower than for a scheme that you arrange for yourself. On the other hand, the choice of ways to invest your AVCs may be more limited than you would like. See Chapter 9 for information about investments.
- **Matched contributions.** Some employers are willing to pay extra towards your pension if you do and so may agree to match your contributions up to a set level – for example, 3 per cent of your pay. This would mean that if you paid extra contributions equal to, say, 2 per cent of your salary, your employer would also pay in 2 per

---

Case Study | **Sam**

Sam, aged 48, is a teacher. She spent over ten years away from paid work while her children were young and then returned to full-time teaching. Currently she is on track to complete 27 years membership of the pension scheme by age 60. Based on her current salary of £34,000 a year, she would get a pension of 27 x 1/80 x £34,000 = £11,475 a year. If she buys five added years, this would boost her pension to 32 x 1/80 x £34,000 = £13,600 a year. She has various options for paying for the added years, for example:

- A single lump sum of just under £34,000. This might be suitable if, say, Sam has just inherited some money
- An increase to her regular monthly contributions. If she paid over 10 years, the cost would be an extra £3,350 a year at her current salary.

cent on your behalf meaning that you benefited from extra contributions of 4 per cent.

- **Taking the benefits.** You could just use the AVC fund that has built up to buy a pension at retirement – and, since April 2006, you could first take up to a quarter of the fund as a tax-free lump sum provided the AVC scheme rules allow this. But the AVC fund might be fairly small in which case you might not get a very good deal on charges when you converted it into a pension. However, the tax rules let you combine the fund from the AVC scheme with the fund or value of your rights from your occupational pension scheme. That means, provided the rules of the occupational and AVC schemes allow it, your tax-free lump sum can be worked out as 25 per cent of the total and paid in all or part from either of the schemes. So you might be able to arrange to take the whole of the AVC proceeds as a tax-free lump sum and draw all the pension from the occupational scheme.

Other ways to make extra contributions

You do not have to use any AVC scheme offered by your employer.

Planning point

Where your employer offers matched contributions when you pay into the in-house AVC scheme, the scheme is likely to be a better way to make extra savings than other types of money purchase pension scheme.

Since April 2006, everyone can pay extra contributions to any type of pension scheme – for example, a personal pension or stakeholder scheme. (Under the pre-April 2006 rules this was not allowed if you earned over £30,000.)

There are also **free-standing AVC schemes** which are basically personal pensions but designed specifically to top up the benefits from your occupational scheme. All these schemes work on a money purchase basis (see Chapter 5) and, since April 2006, there is no fundamental difference between AVC schemes and personal pensions. So you should shop around for whichever gives you the best deal.

Your total contributions to all schemes – including the occupational scheme – need to be within the limits described in Chapter 3 if you are to make the most of the tax reliefs for pension savings.

 Money purchase schemes work like conventional savings and investments, where you pay money in, with the hope that it will grow in the future. See Chapter 5.

At present, Hank earns £30,000 a year and pays 5 per cent of these earnings (£1,500) into his employer's occupational pension scheme. His employer offers a salary sacrifice scheme under which the employer will pay the £1,500 into the pension scheme if Hank accepts a pay cut of £1,400 a year.

The table below compares the position for Hank and his employer if Hank joins the sacrifice scheme. Both gain from the salary sacrifice. Hank still has £1,500 going into the pension scheme for him and also sees his take-home pay rise by £232 despite the £1,400 pay cut. Hank's employer takes over the pension contribution but saves £80 overall through the lower salary and National insurance bills.

Salary sacrifice

There can be advantages for both you and your employer if you receive part of your pay in the form of employer's pension contributions instead of normal pay.

You get income tax relief on contributions you make to your occupational pension scheme but you do not get any relief from National Insurance contributions. By contrast, whatever your employer pays into the scheme on your behalf is a perk of the job on which you pay no income tax and no National

How Hank and his employer benefit from the salary sacrifice scheme

	Before the salary sacrifice	After the salary sacrifice	Gain/loss
Hank's salary	£30,000	£28,600	-£1,400
How much Hank pays into the pension scheme	£1,500	£0	£1,500
Hank's income tax bill	£4,904	£4,926[2]	-£22
Hank's National Insurance (NI) bill	£2,746	£2,592	£154
Hank's take-home pay after deducting pension contribution, tax and NI	£20,850	£21,082	£232
Cost to employer in salary	£30,000	£28,600	£1,400
Cost to employer in pension contribution [1]	£0	£1,500	-£1,500
Employer's NI bill on Hank's salary	£3,196	£3,016	£180
Total cost to the employer	£33,196	£33,116	£80

1 For simplicity, ignoring any other contributions the employer makes on Hank's behalf.

2 The income tax bill rises, because although Hank's pay is now smaller, he no longer has any pension contributions to deduct from his pay before working out the tax.

Insurance. So it's far more tax efficient if your employer pays into the scheme rather than you.

It is also tax-efficient for employers because they pay no National Insurance on money they pay into a pension scheme for their employees but do on money paid out in the form of salaries, bonuses, and so on.

As a result, some employers (for example, BT, Sainsburys and Tesco) are offering **salary sacrifice schemes**. These let you choose to have varying amounts of your pay package in the form of employer's pension contributions instead of normal pay. Even if your employer does not operate such a scheme, they might be willing to set up such an arrangement if you ask. (Salary

> **" There can be advantages for both you and your employer if you receive part of your pay in pension contributions. "**

sacrifice works just as well for payments to, say, a personal pension – see Chapter 5 – instead of an occupational scheme.)

Think carefully before opting for salary sacrifice. It may affect, for example, the state pension you are building up (see Chapter 2) and your entitlement to other state benefits linked to income or earnings. For example, assuming you are not contracted out, giving up part of your pay could reduce your state additional pension (since the amount you get is linked to the average of your pay over your years in the scheme). On the other hand, lower pay could mean, say, you qualify for extra tax credits.

So far, the government has indicated that it is happy for salary sacrifice schemes to exist and has specifically excluded them from tax avoidance legislation but this could change in future.

Planning point

Salary sacrifice schemes save you National Insurance which may mean you can afford to save more for retirement. In addition, your employer might be willing to pass on to you in the form of extra pension contributions some of the National Insurance they save. Check with your employers to see if they run, or would consider, a salary sacrifice scheme.

 For more information from HM Revenue & Customs on taxation and salary sacrifice schemes, see www.hmrc.gov.uk/specialist/sal-sac-question-and-answers.htm

What a combined benefit statement might look like

Your Combined Benefit Statement

When you reach state pension age (65) the DWP expect your total state retirement pension to be	£450 a month
If you stay in the Good2U plc Retirement Benefit Scheme until you reach 65 (the normal pension age for the scheme) your pension is forecast to be	£1,600 a month
Your combined pension from Good2U plc Retirement Benefit Scheme and the state when you are 65 is forecast to be	£2,050 a month

Benefit statements

Benefit statements show an estimate of the pension you might get at normal pension age based on a variety of assumptions. The future could turn out to be different. So it is important to check your statements each year to see if you are still on track for the pension you want and adjust your planning if necessary.

For information about your occupational pension scheme, contact the pension scheme administrator (usually located in the personnel department at work).

KEEPING TRACK

If your employer runs a pension scheme which you are eligible to join, you should be given information about the scheme within two months of starting work.

As a member, you should receive a **yearly benefit statement** estimating the amount of pension you are likely to get from normal pension age. The estimate will be in terms of today's money – in other words, after taking into account the effects of inflation. Some employers issue **combined benefit statements** – see left – which also include an estimate of the amount of state pension you might get at retirement based on your actual National Insurance record (see Chapter 2).

Free leaflets about occupational pension schemes

Reference	Title	From
PM3	Occupational pension schemes - your guide	The Pension Service (www.thepensionservice.gov.uk)
CPF5	Your pension statement	The Pension Service

Personal pensions

So far we have looked at the state pension and company pension schemes. This chapter covers the options available to those who need to make independent arrangements – because they are self-employed, for example, or who want to save more for retirement than their workplace scheme allows.

Personal pension and similar schemes

All the pension schemes described in this chapter are 'money purchase' schemes. They work like conventional savings and investments, where you pay money in aiming for it to grow to a sizeable sum in future.

With these pension schemes, you invest to accumulate a fund of savings. When you come to retire, you use the pension fund that has built up to provide your retirement income. The most common way to do this is to buy an 'annuity'. This is a type of investment where you exchange a lump sum for an income, usually payable for the rest of your life (see page 109).

Chapter 4 described how some of the workplace schemes that your employer might offer work on a money purchase basis. Virtually all the pensions that you arrange for yourself or that are personal to you are also money purchase schemes, including personal pensions, group personal pension schemes, stakeholder schemes, self-invested personal pensions (SIPPs), retirement annuity contracts and free-standing additional voluntary contribution (AVC) schemes.

Since 6 April 2006, the tax rules treat all pension schemes in exactly the same way. In the past the rules were different, which could influence the pension schemes you chose. Now, there is no reason on tax grounds to choose one type of pension scheme over another. The main factors influencing your choice will be factors such as flexibility, charges and investment choice. Options at retirement are also important, but usually you are not tied to one scheme for these and can shop around.

Before April 2006, a lot of employees in occupational pension schemes could not also take out a personal pension or stakeholder scheme. You are now free to top up your pension savings in any way you choose (though individual scheme rules might still limit your choice). But it is still worth checking out any AVC scheme offered by your employer. It might give you a particularly good deal if, say, your employer will match the contributions, the charges are low or it is an 'added years scheme' – see page 93.

WHEN YOU MIGHT USE A PERSONAL PENSION

The main reasons you might take out a personal pension or any of the other money purchase schemes covered in this chapter are:

- If you are self-employed and so have to arrange your own pension savings.
- If you are an employee but there is no occupational scheme, you may be able to join a group personal pension scheme or stakeholder scheme through your workplace. These work in the same way as personal pensions and stakeholder schemes that you arrange for yourself but might have some special features, such as low charges.
- If you belong to an occupational scheme (see Chapter 4) and want to top up the amount you save for retirement. There are now – post-April 2006 – no restrictions on the actual types of pension schemes you can have in addition to belonging to an occupational scheme.
- If you are an employee who decides not to join a pension scheme through your workplace, or there is no workplace scheme.
- If you are an employee taking your own decision to 'contract out' of the state additional pension scheme (see Chapter 6).
- If you are not working but want to save for retirement.
- If you are arranging a scheme for someone else, such as your child. There is no lower limit on the age at which a person can have a pension scheme.

DIFFERENT TYPES OF MONEY PURCHASE SCHEME

Personal pensions and stakeholder schemes

The standard type of pension which you arrange for yourself. Typically they are offered by insurance companies.

You agree either to pay in regular amounts or make single lump sum contributions. Usually you are offered a choice of different investment funds (see Chapter 9). Charges vary greatly from one provider to another. Charges are often lower if you have a large pension fund.

When you want to start your pension, you do not have to stay with the same company but can switch to another provider who may offer a wider range of choices and/or a better deal (see pages 108 and 119).

Your employer may offer a group personal pension scheme (GPSS) through your workplace. This is

Compare different personal pensions and stakeholder schemes using the Financial Services Authority Comparative Tables at www.fsa.gov.uk/tables or 0845 606 1234.

essentially the same as any other personal pension, but your employer may have negotiated some special terms, such as lower charges and might make contributions to the scheme on your behalf.

Stakeholder schemes are simply personal pensions that meet certain conditions – see the table below. You can arrange your own stakeholder scheme. If you are an employee, you may find that your employer offers a scheme through your workplace.

Self-invested personal pension (SIPP)

SIPPs are a type of personal pension offering extra choice and control. Instead of being a single product, typically SIPPs are segregated into their component parts and you can choose different firms to manage each bit:

- **The SIPP wrapper.** You pay for a SIPP manager to handle the administration of your scheme. This may be an insurance company or a specialist SIPP provider.

- **The investments inside the wrapper.** You choose which

Conditions that stakeholder pension schemes must meet

Condition	Details
Capped charges	Charges must be no more than 1.5 per cent a year for the first ten years and 1 per cent a year thereafter. This must cover all the costs of running the scheme, managing your investments and providing information and basic advice. If there is a fee for detailed advice, this must be set out in a separate contract and charged separately
Low and flexible contributions	The minimum contribution must be no higher than £20 whether as a one-off payment or a regular contribution. It's up to you when and how often you pay - you can't be tied in to regular contributions
Portability	You must be able to transfer to another pension scheme without penalty
Simplicity	There must be a default investment option if you don't want to make this choice yourself. The default must be a 'lifestyle fund' where the investments are automatically adjusted as you approach retirement to reduce the risks you take - see Chapter 9 for details

investments to use. Unlike ordinary personal pensions, you are not limited to a small range of funds selected by the scheme provider. You can select funds from different providers and invest direct in things like shares and commercial property. But not all SIPP managers will accept the full range of permitted investments – see Chapter 9.

- **Any other services.** For example, you may wish to receive investment advice or hand over the detailed investment decisions to an investment manager (called a 'discretionary service').

In the past there have been separate charges for each component and these can easily add up to over £1,000 a year. So SIPPs have generally been for wealthy people with, say, a six-figure-plus pension scheme. But recently insurance companies and some other firms have started to offer lower-cost SIPPs where generally the investment choice is more limited and the different components are bundled together with a single set of charges for the whole package.

Retirement annuity contract (RAC)

An old-style personal pension started before July 1988. Although you can no longer start new RACs, you can continue to pay into a scheme you already have.

Before 6 April 2006, different rules applied to RACs than to other personal pensions. But now they are treated exactly the same under the tax rules. However, you may find that providers are slow to change the scheme's own rules, so restrictions might apply, for example, on the age at which you can start your pension. Check with your provider.

Money purchase occupational scheme

See Chapter 4 for details of money purchase occupational schemes and in-house additional voluntary contribution (AVC) schemes.

Free-standing AVC schemes

These schemes are basically the same as personal pensions but, under the pre-April 2006 rules, were designed to let you top up the benefits from an occupational scheme. Now you can use any type of pension scheme to top up your savings, it is doubtful that free-standing AVC schemes will survive as a separate type of scheme. They had not proved popular in any case, because of high charges and pre-April 2006 restrictions on the benefits they could provide.

Small self-administered scheme (SSAS)

SSASs are money purchase occupational schemes for up to 11 members and used, typically, by family companies. The members of an SSAS are usually the people who control the company and often their close relatives. The company is the employer in relation to the scheme. This indirectly gives the members a high degree of control over: how much is paid into the scheme by the employer and/or members, how the scheme is invested (which may include owning the company's premises or lending to the employer – see Chapter 9) and the type and amount of benefits provided by the scheme. However, since all pension schemes are the same under the tax rules from April 2006 onwards, the same advantages can be gained by using a SIPP (see page 102), so it is unclear whether SSAS will continue in future as a distinct type of pension scheme.

Contributions paid into a scheme by an employer on behalf of a member do not count towards a member's limit on contributions that qualify for tax relief. This gives a lot of scope for large contributions to be paid in via the employer. Employers get tax relief on whatever they pay into a scheme provided the

contributions amount to a genuine business expense. This means the contributions for a particular member would have to be compatible with the person's value to the company and the salary they receive.

Executive pension plan (EPP)

An EPP is also an occupational pension scheme but usually tailored to a single member. It is a ready-made package offered by an insurance company with a fairly limited choice of investments. Like an SSAS, an EPP has in the past offered a lot of scope for the employer to make large contributions and so these schemes have generally been used to reward high-flying employees and to build up a large pension over a short space of time.

From 6 April 2006 onwards, all pension schemes are treated the same. An employer can pay contributions into any type of scheme, including an ordinary personal pension, so there is no reason to have a special type of scheme any more. Therefore it is likely that EPPs will disappear.

HOW MUCH PENSION?

You can't know in advance how much pension a money purchase scheme will produce. This depends on:

- The contributions paid in.
- How well the invested contributions grow.
- The charges deducted.
- Annuity rates at the time you start the pension.

CONTRIBUTIONS PAID IN

Who pays what?

With a money purchase occupational scheme, your employer pays in contributions on your behalf and so bears at least part of the cost of providing your pension. Employers can make contributions to any other pension scheme you have, but usually don't.

If you are self-employed or not working, there is no employer to help out, so you alone must normally bear the full cost of providing your pension.

There are no restrictions on other people paying into your pension

Case Study Arif

Arif works for himself as a journalist. He pays a lump sum of £5,000 into his personal pension. This is treated as a net contribution. The pension provider then claims tax relief from HM Revenue & Customs and adds it to Arif's scheme. When the basic rate is 22 per cent, this means £1,410 tax relief is added bringing Arif's gross contribution to £6,410. (£1,410 is 22 per cent of £6,410.) Arif is a higher rate taxpayer. Assuming the higher tax rate is 40 per cent, this means Arif can claim a further 18 per cent of £6,410 = £1,154 in tax relief through his tax return. In total £6,410 has gone into Arif's pension scheme at a cost to Arif of just £5,000 – £1,154 = £3,846.

scheme for you. For example, your spouse or partner could pay into your scheme.

Contributions must normally be in the form of money (for example, paid by cheque, direct debit or bank transfer) but you can transfer shares you have acquired through some types of employee share scheme at work (SAYE share option scheme and share incentive plan) direct to your pension scheme within 90 days of getting the shares.

Jargon buster

Net An amount after deduction of tax or tax relief.

Gross An amount before deduction of tax or tax relief. It equals the net amount plus the tax or tax relief deducted.

Tax relief on contributions

Chapter 3 explained the tax advantages of saving through a pension scheme including tax relief on contributions (see pages 60-5).

105

Case Study **Lyn and Wies**

Lyn and Wies have a family. At present Lyn stays home to look after the children and they rely on Wies' earnings. Although Lyn is not earning, they both feel it is important that she carries on saving for retirement, so Lyn has taken out a stakeholder pension scheme and Wies helps her to pay regular amounts into it. Lyn is a non-taxpayer. She pays £50 into her stakeholder pension scheme. This is treated as a contribution from which tax relief at the basic rate has been deducted. The pension provider claims the relief of £14.10 from HM Revenue & Customs and adds it to her scheme. So, at a cost to Lyn of £50, £64.10 has gone into her scheme.

With most schemes, except occupational schemes (see page 77), contributions paid in by you, or by someone else other than your employer, are treated as 'net' contributions from which tax relief at the basic rate has already been deducted. Everyone gets this relief, regardless of whether they are a taxpayer or the rate of tax they pay. So for non-taxpayers and starting-rate taxpayers, the tax relief is like a bonus added to the scheme – see Case study Lyn and Wies, above.

Where you pay contributions in to your own scheme, you get extra relief if you are a higher-rate taxpayer. Normally you do this by claiming through your tax return. If you don't get a tax return, contact your tax office.

If you pay into somebody else's scheme for them, the basic rate relief is added to their scheme as normal. But you would not be able to claim any further tax relief even if you were a higher-rate taxpayer.

Tax relief on contributions to retirement annuity contracts (old-style personal pensions started before July 1988) is given differently. You pay 'gross' contributions and claim all the tax relief through your tax return or tax office.

Like all other types of pension scheme, retirement annuity contracts are now covered by the post-April-2006 rules and treated the same for tax purposes as any other scheme. But there is a small hangover from the pre-April-2006 rules. The old rules allowed you to treat a contribution paid in one tax year as if you had paid it in the previous tax year – called 'carry back'. You then got tax relief at the rates for the earlier year. You had up to 31 January following the end of the tax year in which you paid the contribution to make an election to use the carry back rule. This means you still have until 31 January 2007 to decide whether you want to have a contribution you paid in 2005-6 treated as if you had paid it in 2004-5. This would be worth doing if, say, you paid tax at a higher rate in the earlier year.

INVESTMENT GROWTH

It is important to realise that the investment decisions you make will have a big impact on how much pension you eventually receive. Analysts reckon that the major influence on your return is not the individual funds you choose but the balance between broad types of investments, called asset classes. These include cash (deposits where your money earns interest), bonds (loans to governments or companies), property (investments in commercial properties, either directly or by owning shares in companies that run them) and equities (shares in companies). The return you might get from each of these varies according to the risk involved. Cash is the 'safest', but also earns the lowest return. Equities, on the other hand, offer the prospect of a higher return but carry the risk of losses. The best strategy for most people is to keep a spread of different types of investment. You can achieve this by choosing a mix of different investment funds or a single fund that automatically holds a mix of different assets. For full information about investing your pension scheme, see Chapter 9.

CHARGES

Charges can have a big impact on the value of your pension fund – see the table below. For example, if you start to save regularly from age 20 and investment growth averaged 7 per cent a year, each £1,000 of your fund before charges could be reduced by almost a quarter to £770 if charges were just 1 per cent a year. The impact of charges is greatest the longer your money is invested because you lose not just the charges themselves but also the future growth you would have had on that amount.

The effect charges can have on your pension fund

	Value of each £1,000 of your pension fund in today's money [1] by age of 65 if you start to save regularly from age:			
	20	30	40	50
Before deducting charges	£1,000	£1,000	£1,000	£1,000
After charges of 0.5% a year	£875	£905	£933	£961
After charges of 1% a year	£770	£821	£873	£924
After charges of 1.5% a year	£680	£747	£817	£889
After charges of 2% a year	£603	£682	£766	£856

1 Assuming the pension fund grows by 7 per cent a year before charges, inflation averages 2.5 per cent a year and you increase your contributions each year in line with average earnings (assumed to average 4 per cent a year).

YOUR CHOICES AT RETIREMENT

How you draw your benefits

You may be able to take part of the fund that has built up as a tax-free lump sum (see page 118). The rest is normally used to provide a pension using:

● An annuity (see opposite), and/or
● Income withdrawal (see page 114).

If you belong to a money purchase occupational scheme, the scheme might normally arrange a scheme pension by buying an annuity for you, but it must give you the option of shopping around for your own lifetime annuity if you want to.

Starting your pension

Under the tax rules, you can normally start your pension at any age from 50

(rising to 55 by 6 April 2010) onwards, but sooner if you have to retire early because of ill health.

In practice, your ability to start drawing your pension at an early age – whether through ill health or otherwise – is likely to be limited since, with money purchase schemes, the earlier you start your pension, the smaller it will be because:

● Generally, fewer contributions will have been paid in.
● The pension fund has had less time to grow.
● The annuity rate determining the pension you get will be lower, reflecting the fact that the pension has to be paid out for longer.

Conversely, the later you leave starting your pension, in general the larger the pension you'll get.

You do not actually have to retire in order to start drawing your pension.

Increases to your pension after it starts

For pensions starting since 6 April 2005, there is no requirement for the pension from any money purchase scheme to increase automatically (for example, in line with inflation). It is up to you to decide whether you want this feature.

Since 6 April 2006, the tax rules let you take a tax-free lump sum from any type of money purchase scheme. In general it is worth taking the largest possible amount, as the lump sum is tax-free, whereas the pension is taxable. See page 118 for more details.

USING AN ANNUITY TO PROVIDE YOUR PENSION

How annuities work

Annuities are a special type of investment where you pay a lump sum (in this case, all or part of your pension fund) and in return get an income either for the rest of your life (a 'lifetime annuity') or for a specified period (a 'short-term annuity').

The 'annuity rate' tells you the amount of income you will get each year in return for your lump sum. Generally, it is expressed as so many pounds a year for each £10,000 you invest. For example, an annuity rate of £650 would mean you get £650 a year for each £10,000 invested. If you invested £30,000 you would get £30,000/10,000 x £650 = £1,950 a year.

The annuity rate at the time you buy the annuity determines the income you will get for the rest of your life with a lifetime annuity or for the whole annuity period in the case of a short-term annuity. This does not necessarily mean you will get the same income every year. Some types of annuity do provide the same income year-in, year-out. But you can choose others that give you built-in increases or where the income fluctuates up and down.

In the past, the usual course has been to use your pension fund to buy a lifetime annuity. This gives you the reassurance that you will continue to receive a pension for the rest of your

Choices by age 75

Whatever choices you make earlier, by age 75 you must use your remaining pension fund either to buy a lifetime annuity or for income withdrawal (see page 114).

life, however long you live. In this way, conventional annuities are a sort of insurance against living longer than expected – see the box below.

The table on page 110 sets out the main factors that determine the lifetime annuity rate you'll be offered. One of the most important is life expectancy. As discussed in the Introduction, average life expectancy in the UK has been steadily increasing and is expected to rise further. As a

Annuities as a type of insurance

With normal life insurance, you take out cover against dying prematurely. Your premiums are paid into a pool with those from lots of other people. The pool pays out to the survivors of those people who do die young; the people who survive get nothing but have had the peace of mind of knowing that the life insurance would have paid out if need be.

Lifetime annuities work in a very similar way. The money you invest is pooled with that from lots of other people. The average life expectancy of every one in the pool determines how much is paid out in yearly pensions. The people who live longer than expected get a bigger share of the pool over the years; the people who die younger than expected, get a smaller share but have had the peace of mind of knowing that their pension would have carried on had they survived longer.

Main factors determining your annuity rate

Factor	How it affects the rate	Why it has an effect
Personal factors		
Your age	Older – higher rate Younger – lower rate	The younger you are, the longer your pension is likely to be paid out so the more it is expected to cost in total (and so the less you get each year)
Your gender	Man – higher rate Woman – lower rate	Women tend on average to live longer than men, so their pensions generally cost more
Your state of health	Poor health – higher rate Good health – lower rate	Someone in poor health will probably live for a shorter period than someone in good health, so their pension will be cheaper in total
Your lifestyle	Unhealthy (such as smoking, heavy manual job, and so on) – higher rate Healthy – lower rate	Someone who smokes, say, will probably live for a shorter period than someone with a healthy lifestyle so their pension will be cheaper in total
Economic factors		
Long-term interest rates	High interest rates – higher rate Low interest rates – lower rate	Pensions are funded partly by the money you invest and partly by the interest earned when that money is invested
Average life expectancy	Falling life expectancy – higher rate Increasing life expectancy – lower rate	The longer people live, the longer their pensions have to be paid out and so the more they cost in total

result, annuity rates have fallen dramatically over the last 15 years or so. For example, in 1990, a man aged 65 could invest his savings in an annuity to provide a pension of around £1,600 a year for each £10,000 invested. By 2005, the amount had more than halved to just £700 a year. This huge fall has caused many people to question whether annuities offer value for money any more and is one of the reasons for the great interest in alternatives to conventional annuities.

When to buy an annuity

Lifetime annuity rates reflect the cost of providing a pension year after year

Jargon buster

Short-term annuity An investment where you swap a lump sum for an income paid out for a specified period of time. At the end of the period, the income stops. You cannot normally get your original investment back as lump sum.

Life expectancy The number of years someone of a given age is on average expected to live based on statistical evidence.

for as long as you live. So the older you are when you buy, the larger the yearly pension you get for any given sum invested – see the table below. This contributes towards giving you a bigger pension if you retire later (see page 108).

Coping with inflation

The most basic type of lifetime annuity is a level annuity. It pays out the same income every year. The main

drawback is that inflation eats into the buying power of your money over time (see page 23). For example, if you start with a level pension of £10,000 a year, after 10 years it will buy only the same as £7,800 today if inflation averages even a modest 2.5 per cent a year.

There are several ways you can plan to protect yourself against the effects of inflation. You could stick with a level annuity but save some of the income during the early years and use it to top up your pension later on. Maybe you could top up using other sources savings. Alternatively, you could choose an annuity with built-in increases. These are the main types:

- **Escalating annuity.** This increases by a set percentage – for example, 3 per cent – each year. If inflation is lower, your income goes up by more than enough to retain the buying power of your money. If inflation is higher, you still lose some buying power.

How annuity rates vary with age

| Age when you | Annuity rate | |
buy annuity	Men	Women
50	£516	£480
55	£564	£516
60	£624	£564
65	£720	£624
70	£864	£720
75	£1,032	£828

- **RPI-linked annuity.** This changes (up or down) each year in line with inflation so the buying power of your pension remains constant. 'RPI' stands for Retail Prices Index changes in which are the most commonly used measure of price inflation in the UK.
- **LPI annuity.** 'LPI' stands for 'limited price indexation'. The income from the annuity increases each year in line with the RPI up to a capped amount – say, 3 per cent or 5 per cent a year. In the past, some pension schemes had to provide LPI annuities, but since 6 April 2005 onwards this is no longer a requirement.

The cost of increasing annuities

The main drawback with increasing annuities is that the starting income is much lower than the amount you get from a level annuity. Consider, for example, the position for a man aged 65. If he buys an annuity escalating at 3 per cent a year, the starting income is 30 per cent lower than the £720 a year he would get from a level annuity. It will take 12 years before the income from the escalating annuity catches up and 23 years before it has paid out as much in total as the level annuity. With the RPI-linked annuity, the starting income is 35 per cent lower, but how long it takes to catch up depends on how inflation turns out in future. With a low rate of inflation, it would take

many years. But if inflation returned to the high levels seen in the past (a peak of 27 per cent a year in 1975) the income would catch up very quickly.

Providing for a partner

If you have a spouse, civil partner or other partner who will be dependent wholly or partly on your pension, one way to ensure they could manage if you die first is to choose a joint-life-last-survivor annuity. This continues paying out an income until the second of you dies. See Chapter 8 for further details.

Getting value for money

If it worries you that dying soon after your pension starts would mean getting back less in pension than the amount you invested, consider a 'guarantee'. This is an assurance that the pension will be paid for a minimum period (up to ten years) even if you die within that period. You can nominate who would receive the continuing income. Your starting income is reduced by an amount that depends on your age, the age of your partner if it's a joint annuity and the length of the guarantee.

Another newer option that might appeal to you for the same reason is 'annuity protection'. With this, a lump sum can be paid out to anyone you nominate if you die before age 75. The sum is equal to the purchase price of the annuity less the value of the pension paid out so far. Tax at 35 per cent in 2006-7 is deducted before the sum is paid out. Again your starting income is reduced.

For more information about benefits payable on death, see Chapter 8.

If you have specific reasons to think that your life expectancy is shorter than average – for example, because you are in poor health or smoke – some annuity providers offer 'impaired life annuities' which pay a higher-than-normal pension.

With investment-linked annuities, instead of buying a predictable pension, the lifetime annuity provides an income whose value is linked to an underlying fund of stock-market investments. Your hope is that the income will be higher than from a conventional annuity, but the income you get will change from year to year as the value of the investments in the fund rises and falls. The income may even fall. You need to have sufficient income either from the annuity or

Inflation

You are taking a big gamble with your retirement income if you take no steps to protect yourself against the effects of inflation. Options include saving in early retirement to top up your pension later on or choosing an annuity which increases each year.

other sources to be able to cope with these fluctuations.

If you think that annuity rates might improve later on, you could consider a short-term annuity. You use part of your pension fund to buy an annuity lasting up to five years. The rest of your pension fund remains invested. At the end of that time, you can buy another short-term annuity if you want to again lasting up to five years. Any short-term annuity must come to an end before you reach age 75.

Planning point

Some options involve leaving part or all of your pension fund invested or linking your annuity income to investment performance. You generally need to invest in relatively risky share-based investments that offer the chance of a higher return if you are to beat the deal you would have had from buying a conventional lifetime annuity. For more information, see Mortality drag, page 117.

USING INCOME WITHDRAWAL

Income withdrawal means leaving your pension fund invested and drawing a pension straight from the fund instead of buying an annuity. It is a very flexible way of providing a pension but involves extra costs and risks.

At any time, you can stop using income withdrawal and use your remaining pension fund to buy a lifetime annuity instead. But, unlike the pre-April 2006 regime, you no longer have to buy an annuity by age 75 – you can instead carry on with income withdrawal.

❝ To make income withdrawal worthwhile, you need to invest in share-based investments that are likely to give a higher return. ❞

Income withdrawal before age 75

The tax rules restrict the maximum pension you can have to 120 per cent of the lifetime annuity you could otherwise have bought. For this purpose, the annuity is defined as a level single-life annuity without guarantee for someone of your age and gender. The government publishes the rates to be used.

The maximum income is set for five years at a time and recalculated at every fifth anniversary using your remaining pension fund and your age at the date of the review. The

---

Case Study Geoff

Geoff, 65, has a remaining pension fund of £100,000 after taking part as a tax-free lump sum. The annuity rate for a single-life level annuity without guarantee for a man of his age is £720. If he opts for income withdrawal, the maximum income he can draw is 120% x £720 x £100,000/10,000 = £8,640 a year.

---

reviews are a safeguard to prevent you running down your pension fund too fast.

Up to the maximum, you choose how much income you want to withdraw each year. Unlike the earlier rules for income withdrawal, under the post-April 2006 regime, there is no minimum income that you must have. This means you could just take the tax-free lump sum and put off drawing any pension at all until later.

Income withdrawal from age 75

Once you reach age 75 you must either buy a lifetime annuity if you haven't already done so or opt for a more restricted form of income withdrawal called an 'alternatively secured pension' (ASP).

With ASP, the maximum pension you can have is 70 per cent of the lifetime annuity you could otherwise have bought. The maximum limit must be reviewed every year. But the annuity rate used is always that for a person of your gender aged 75,

> ## Case Study | Ghalib
>
> Ghalib, 75, has a remaining pension fund of £100,000 after taking part as a tax-free lump sum. The annuity rate for a single-life level annuity without guarantee for a man of 75 is £1,032. If he opts for income withdrawal, the maximum income he can draw is 70% x £1,032 x £100,000/10,000 = £7,224 a year.

regardless of your actual age at the time of review.

Up to the maximum, you choose how much income you want to draw each year. Again, there is no minimum income you must have, so you could put off drawing any pension until later.

Advantages of income withdrawal

Income withdrawal gives you a lot of flexibility. For example, you can:

- Vary the amount of income you draw each year. For example, you might draw a low pension in the early years while you are still doing some paid work and increase the pension as you retire more fully.
- Just take the tax-free lump sum (for example, so you can pay off your mortgage) but put off drawing the pension until you need it later on.
- Provide for your partner or other dependants because, if you die first, they can use your remaining pension fund to provide pensions –

see Chapter 8. Therefore, by drawing a lower pension yourself, you can increase the amount available for their pensions.

- Leave a lump sum to your heirs if you die before age 75, because your remaining fund can be paid out to them though this will be taxed. By drawing a lower pension, you can increase the amount you leave but, if you are thought to be deliberately using your pension scheme for inheritance rather than pension purposes, there could be extra tax to pay. See Chapter 8 for more details.
- Keep control of the way your pension fund is invested. This may be important if you like to select your own investments or have strong ethical beliefs. For more information about investments, see Chapter 9.

Income withdrawal also offers an alternative for people who are unable to use annuities because of their religious beliefs - for example, the Plymouth Brethren, who view annuities as a form of gambling which is unacceptable in their faith.

You might be tempted to use income withdrawal if you think buying a lifetime annuity looks poor value, but read about the drawbacks below before making up your mind on this point.

115

Alternatively secured pension A type of income withdrawal from age 75 where the maximum pension you can draw is based on cautious assumptions to guard against your pension fund running out during your lifetime and other restrictions apply.

" Although share-based investments have tended to produce significantly higher returns than safer investments over the long term, their value can go down as well as up. "

Drawbacks of income withdrawal

Once you have bought a lifetime annuity, there are usually no more charges for providing your pension. With income withdrawal, investment management charges continue for as long as your pension fund remains invested and there are administration charges for example for carrying out the regular reviews. These all add up and make income withdrawal uneconomic if you have only a small pension fund.

In general, to make income withdrawal worthwhile, you need to invest in share-based investments. This is for two reasons:

Planning point

Because of the charges and the fact that your pension can fall as well as rise, income withdrawal will generally be suitable only if you have a six-figure pension fund and/or substantial other retirement income.

- As noted on page 110, the income from an annuity is funded partly from the money you use to buy the annuity and partly from the interest that money earns by being invested. The annuity provider puts the money into fairly safe investments that provide a low but predictable income. If, using income withdrawal, you are to get a higher income than the annuity could provide, you need to choose investments that are likely to give a higher return.
- As discussed on page 109, annuities are a type of insurance. By choosing income withdrawal, you lose this insurance element and your investments need to produce extra return to compensate for the loss if you are to beat the income from an annuity (see Mortality drag, opposite).

Although share-based investments have tended to produce significantly higher returns than safer investments over the long term (see Chapter 9), their value can go down as well as up. If your pension fund investments fall

Mortality drag

Mortality drag refers to the loss of a cross-subsidy you would have had if you had bought a conventional lifetime annuity. The income you get from a conventional lifetime annuity is based on the average life expectancy for a pool of people of your age at the time you buy the annuity. Some of the people in the pool will die early. As they do, money that would otherwise have paid their pensions becomes available to help pay the pensions of everyone left in the pool. In this way, there is a cross-subsidy from the people who die young to the people who live longer.

If you put off buying an annuity until later, these early-death people have already dropped out of the annuity pool. Moreover, the survivors who are left are now expected to live to a higher average age – for example, average life expectancy for men aged 60 is 23 years to age 83, but average life expectancy for men aged 70 is 15 years to age 85.

These factors have a dampening effect on the annuity rate, so that the later you leave buying an annuity, the poorer the deal you get. If you never buy an annuity, you lose out on the cross-subsidy altogether and must rely purely on your own investments to fund your own pension without any insurance element at all.

Personal pensions

in value, the maximum pension you can have will usually also fall.

Another drawback to consider is the inheritance tax treatment of income withdrawal. The government is very clear that the special tax treatment of pension schemes is designed to encourage you to provide yourself with retirement income. Using pension schemes to pass on an inheritance tax efficiently is considered an abuse of the tax reliefs. In Budget 2006, the government confirmed that where you opt for income withdrawal from age 75, any of your pension fund left at death will be subject to inheritance tax unless it is used to provide pensions for your dependents or bequeathed to charity. If you have opted for income withdrawal before age 75 and die, inheritance tax will apply only if you had taken decisions deliberately aimed at boosting the amount you could leave to non-dependent heirs – for example, by failing to draw the maximum possible pension when terminally ill. See Chapter 8 for more details.

117

TAKING A TAX-FREE LUMP SUM

Since 6 April 2006, the tax rules allow you to take a tax-free lump sum from any type of money purchase scheme (though a scheme's own rules will not necessarily permit this). The maximum lump sum is the lower of:

- A quarter of the fund that has built up, and
- A quarter of the standard lifetime allowance (see page 72) less the value of any benefits you have already taken.

In general, it is worth taking the largest possible lump sum even if you need income, because the lump sum is tax-free whereas the pension is taxable. You could invest the lump sum in, say, a 'purchased life annuity'. This works in the same way as the

Case Study Fiona

Fiona, 71, has a pension fund of £50,000. The level annuity rate for a woman of her age is £752, so Fiona could convert the whole fund into a pension of £50,000/10,000 x £752 = £3,760 a year. After basic rate tax this would give her an after-tax pension of £2,933.

Alternatively, Fiona could take a quarter of the fund as a tax-free lump sum. The remaining pension fund of £37,500 would buy a pension of £2,200 after tax. With the tax-free £12,500, she could buy a purchased life annuity. The best rate she can get is £713 giving her a before-tax income of £12,500/10,000 x £713 = £891 a year. But over four-fifths of this counts as return of her original lump sum leaving only £154 to be taxed. After tax, the net income is £860 a year. Her total net income from both annuities is £2,200 + £860 = £3,060 (an increase of £127 a year).

Jargon buster

Purchased life annuity An annuity you choose to buy with money other than a pension fund. Part of each payment you receive counts as return of your original investment and is tax-free. The rest is taxable.

annuities already described except it is taxed differently: part of each payment you receive is treated as return of your original investment and is tax-free; the rest is taxable.

Your lifetime allowance is a value of benefits (pensions, tax-free lump sums and payments to your survivors if you die) that can be drawn from all of your pension schemes without a special tax charge being payable. For further details see Chapter 3.

SHOPPING AROUND FOR THE RIGHT SCHEME

Where to get information

To compare personal pensions, stakeholder schemes or pension annuities, check out the Financial Services Authority (FSA) Comparative Tables at www.fsa.gov.uk/tables or phone the FSA for a print out.

See articles and surveys in specialist magazines, such as *Money Management* (available from newsagents) and *Which?* (available in public reference libraries). Personal finance websites (such as www.moneyfacts.co.uk) and pages in newspapers often have tables comparing annuity rates.

Get information about particular schemes or annuities direct from providers – many have websites. Look out for the 'key features document'. This is required by the FSA. It gives information about a product in a standard format designed to explain the main features clearly and make it easy to compare one scheme with another.

Some specialist independent financial advisers have websites where you can check out and compare current annuity rates (see, for example, www.annuity-bureau.co.uk and www.annuitydirect.co.uk).

Shopping around when you start to save

Check out the following details before committing yourself to a particular pension scheme:

- **What's on offer at work?** If you can join an occupational scheme, this will usually be the best way to save for retirement – see Chapter 4. If there is a group personal pension scheme or stakeholder scheme at work, will your employer pay into it and/or does it have any special features? If so, it may be a better option that a scheme you arrange for yourself.
- **The provider's credentials.** Is the provider 'authorised' by the FSA? Find out by checking the FSA Register at www.fsa.gov.uk/register or phoning the FSA. If it is not authorised, report the firm to the FSA and do not do business.
- **Contributions.** Is there a minimum contribution – is it too high? Are you happy to pay regularly or do you

Jargon buster

Financial Services Authority (FSA) Body established by law to regulate the provision of, and advice about, most financial products and services in the UK. It also publishes a wide range of information in print and on its website at www.fsa.gov.uk.

Authorised Means a firm has been checked out by the Financial Services Authority and is allowed to conduct financial business in the UK. Provided you deal with an authorised firm, you benefit from consumer protection - for example, complaints procedures and a compensation scheme if things go wrong.

Open market option Your option to shop around and buy an annuity from any provider of your choice rather than sticking with the provider with whom you have built up your pension fund.

Checking out the charges

The key features document includes an illustration of the pension you might get by a selected age based on various assumptions and shows the effect of charges on the value of your pension fund. Look for the statement that says something like: 'by age 65, charges would reduce the assumed growth of your pension fund from 7 per cent to 5.8 per cent'. In this example, charges have reduced the value of the fund by 7% – 5.8% = 1.2%. This is called the 'reduction in yield' and is very useful because it rolls up into a single figure the effect of all the different charges applying to the scheme. You can compare the reduction in yield for different schemes to see which is most expensive. For example, a scheme with a reduction in yield of 1.9 per cent would be more expensive than one with the reduction in yield of 1.2 per cent.

What do the charges add up to in total? (See Checking out the charges box, left.) Are they higher than for other schemes? If you have to pay over the odds, are you getting something extra in return? If not, avoid high-charging schemes.

- **When can you start your pension?** Do you have to specify a particular age in advance? If so, can you change that age without penalty? Can you draw just part of your pension? Many schemes are set up as clusters of lots of mini-schemes, giving you the flexibility to cash in just part at a time.

Shopping around when you want to buy an annuity

All money purchase schemes must give you the option of shopping around for a lifetime annuity when you want your pension to start – this is called an 'open market option'. In general, it makes sense to use the option because annuity rates can vary greatly from one provider to another and the firm with whom you built up your pension scheme will not necessarily be the best buy when it comes to annuities. There are two situations when this might not hold:

want the flexibility to vary your contributions? Check how much flexibility a scheme offers and, if it requires regular contributions, whether there are penalties if you miss payments. Stakeholder schemes must be flexible and penalty free.

- **Investments.** Do you want to choose your own investments? If so, you probably need to look at self-invested personal pensions (or if you run your own business, a small self-administered scheme). Bigger choice usually means higher charges, so don't choose a scheme with more options than you need. See Chapter 9 for information on investments.
- **Charges.** What charges are there – admin fee, yearly charge, other? Beware of flat-rate charges that can eat heavily into small contributions.

- If you belong to a money purchase occupational scheme that arranges scheme pensions for its members. Because the occupational scheme can buy annuities in bulk, it may be able to get better annuity terms than you can arrange for yourself.

- If the provider with whom you have built up your pension scheme offers a 'guaranteed annuity rate'. This is fairly common with schemes taken out before the 1990s. The scheme may have guaranteed that, at retirement, your pension would be based on an annuity rate no less than a specified amount. As annuity rates have generally halved over the last 15 years, some of these rates now look high and are impossible to beat by shopping around.

Not all providers offer a full range of choices at retirement. For example, if you want a short-term annuity or income withdrawal, you may have to switch to a specialist provider.

GETTING ADVICE

You may want help deciding how much to save, which options to choose and/or picking the best products and providers. There are three types of adviser to go to:

- **Provider/tied adviser.** Can advise on only the products of a single provider. Contact the product provider.
- **Multi-tied adviser.** The adviser can recommend products from a limited range of different providers. This is usually the case if you go to, say, a bank or building society for advice.
- **Independent financial adviser/ whole of market adviser.** The adviser can select the best product for you from the full range on the market.

Paying for advice: fees vs commission

	Commission	Fees
When you pay	• Cost spread over many years since you pay gradually through the scheme charges • But balance may have to be paid in a single lump sum through penalty charges if you stop or transfer the scheme in the early years	Paid in a single lump sum (which may be several hundred pounds) when advice received
Impact on advice	Risk that a bad adviser is swayed by commission to recommend: • products or providers that pay higher commission • you invest more than needed • you switch schemes often	Less risk of advice being influenced by method or amount of payment

Financial products - a shopper's guide

1 Do your homework. Work out roughly what you need and find out broadly what's available
2 Gather together information you'll need - for example, proof of your earnings, state pension forecast, benefit statements
3 Deal only with firms or advisers who are authorised. Check the FSA Register (www.fsa.gov.uk/register)
4 Read the literature you get, especially key features documents and their replacements due from 2007, which will be branded 'Key Facts'
5 Ask questions about anything you do not understand
6 Get advice if you do not feel confident making a decision on your own
7 Check the sort of advice an adviser offers and how they will be paid
8 Avoid advisers who do not ask enough questions to understand your needs and circumstances
9 If a deal sounds too good to be true, avoid it
10 Keep a file of all the information - product literature, notes of phone conversations and meetings, letters, and so on - that formed the basis of your decision. You'll need these details if you later have a complaint (see Chapter 10).

An adviser may be paid in two ways. Commonly they receive commission from the provider whose product they sell to you. You pay the commission indirectly through the charges for the product. Whole of market advisers who want to call themselves 'independent' must offer you the option of paying for the advice through a fee paid direct to the adviser.

KEEPING TRACK

With all money purchase schemes, you should receive a statement once a year setting out in today's money, the pension you are expected to get by a specified age based on various assumptions. The statement will be very similar to that described at the end of Chapter 4 (see page 98) and, if it is a combined statement, will also include a forecast of the state pension you may get from state pension age.

Free leaflets about occupational pension schemes

Reference	Title	From
PM4	Personal pensions - your guide	The Pension Service
PM5	Pensions for the self-employed - your guide	The Pension Service
PM8	Stakeholder pensions - your guide	The Pension Service
CPF5	Your pension statement	The Pension Service
CRED0048bp	Income withdrawal - a retirement option for you?	Financial Services Authority

Contracting out

'Contracting out' is a process whereby you opt to give up some of your state pension (S2P/SERPS) and build up a private pension instead. You either pay lower National Insurance contributions or get a rebate of part of the National Insurance you have paid, which is invested in the private pension.

Contracting out of S2P/SERPS

Chapter 2 described the pension you might build up through the state additional pension scheme. You can contract out of this part of the state scheme and instead build up some pension through an occupational scheme (see Chapter 4) or a personal pension/stakeholder scheme (see Chapter 5).

This chapter describes how contracting out works and how to decide whether it is a good idea for you.

WHEN CAN YOU CONTRACT OUT?

You must be an employee eligible for the state additional pension scheme in order to contract out of it (see page 42). For example, contracting out is not an option if you are an employee earning less than the lower earnings limit (£84 a week in 2006-7) or you are self-employed.

Jargon buster

Contracting out Giving up some state additional pension and building up a pension instead through either an occupational scheme or a personal pension/stakeholder scheme. Part of the National Insurance you and your employer pay which would have gone towards the state scheme is used to build up the alternative pension.

You can contract in and out as many times as you like. Generally, it's a good idea to check on a year-by-year basis whether you are likely to be better off in the state scheme or contracted out.

WHAT HAPPENS?

Three things happen when you contract out:

- You either pay less National Insurance or part of your National Insurance is refunded.
- You give up some state pension.
- You build up a replacement pension through an occupational scheme or personal pension.

Deciding whether or not contracting out is a good idea means weighing up these three factors. The situation varies depending on the route by which you are contracted out: occupational scheme or personal pension. In some occupational schemes that are already contracted-out, you don't have much choice.

CONTRACTING OUT THROUGH AN OCCUPATIONAL SCHEME

Some occupational pension schemes work on a contracted-out basis, so when you join the scheme you are normally automatically contracted out. You can't take the decision to contract out in isolation from your decision to join.

Reduced National Insurance contributions

If you are contracted-out through an occupational scheme, you pay less in National Insurance contributions. The reduction is the amount that would have gone towards the state pension you would otherwise have been building up. In 2006-7, the reduction is 1.6 per cent of your earnings between the primary threshold (£97 a week) and the upper earnings limit (£645 a week). The table right gives examples of the saving you make.

If your occupational scheme is a contributory scheme, the amount you must pay in contributions may exceed the amount you save in National Insurance contributions.

Your employer also pays less National Insurance. The government sets the reductions at the level it reckons, based on assumptions, should be enough to compensate for the loss of state pension.

Giving up S2P

The table on page 127 gives a rough guide to the yearly amount of state

Why some contracted-out people get a residual state second pension

From April 2002, the previous state additional pension scheme, SERPS, was replaced by S2P. The new scheme is more generous than SERPS. However, to keep things simple, the reduction in National Insurance on contracting out continues to be set in the same way as it was under SERPS. This means the National Insurance reduction is not enough to compensate for the loss of S2P and so you still get some additional pension equal to the difference between the S2P you would get if in the scheme and the SERPS you would have had if SERPS had continued.

pension you would be giving up if you contracted out during 2006-7. It is based on various assumptions and the

How National Insurance is reduced

Your earnings £ a year	Amount you pay if you are in the state additional scheme £ a year	Amount you pay if contracted out £ a year	Reduction in your National Insurance in 2006-7
£5,000	£0.00	£0.00	£0.00
£10,000	£546.15	£466.71	£79.44
£20,000	£1,647.15	£1,406.71	£239.44
£30,000	£2,746.15	£2,346.71	£399.44
£40,000	£3,200.15	£2,744.07	£456.08
£50,000	£3,300.15	£2,844.07	£456.08

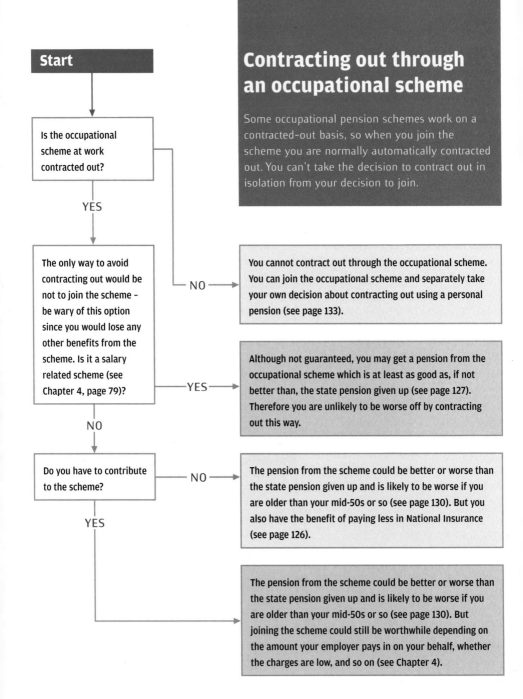

Start

Contracting out through an occupational scheme

Some occupational pension schemes work on a contracted-out basis, so when you join the scheme you are normally automatically contracted out. You can't take the decision to contract out in isolation from your decision to join.

Is the occupational scheme at work contracted out?

YES

The only way to avoid contracting out would be not to join the scheme – be wary of this option since you would lose any other benefits from the scheme. Is it a salary related scheme (see Chapter 4, page 79)?

NO

Do you have to contribute to the scheme?

YES

NO → You cannot contract out through the occupational scheme. You can join the occupational scheme and separately take your own decision about contracting out using a personal pension (see page 133).

YES → Although not guaranteed, you may get a pension from the occupational scheme which is at least as good as, if not better than, the state pension given up (see page 127). Therefore you are unlikely to be worse off by contracting out this way.

NO → The pension from the scheme could be better or worse than the state pension given up and is likely to be worse if you are older than your mid-50s or so (see page 130). But you also have the benefit of paying less in National Insurance (see page 126).

The pension from the scheme could be better or worse than the state pension given up and is likely to be worse if you are older than your mid-50s or so (see page 130). But joining the scheme could still be worthwhile depending on the amount your employer pays in on your behalf, whether the charges are low, and so on (see Chapter 4).

actual loss of pension may be different in your own case. In particular, if you reached age 16 before 1978 (when the state additional pension scheme started), the amount of state pension you give up will be larger than the amounts shown.

If you refer back to page 45, you can see that the state additional pension you build up if you are in the scheme is worked out by dividing your earnings into bands. When you contract out through an occupational pension scheme, if you earn less than the upper limit of the Band 2 earnings (£28,764 in 2006-7), you do not give up all your state additional pension – you still get a residual amount. The reason for this is a bit technical. The table, right, takes this residual pension into account and shows the amount of state pension you actually give up.

Pension from a contracted-out salary-related scheme

Having taken the decision to contract out, your employer must run an occupational scheme which offers at least 90 per cent of the members of the scheme benefits which are at least as good as or better than the benefits from a 'reference scheme'. (You may be required to contribute towards the scheme.) The main reference scheme terms are:

- A retirement pension from a normal pension age of 65 equal to 1/80th of earnings for each year of service up to a maximum of 40. Earnings are

Estimated state pension given up (2006-7)

Your earnings £ a year	S2P for year if you are in the state scheme £ a year	S2P given up if you contract out £ a year	Residual S2P you still get if contracted out £ a year
£5,000	£66.38	£2.58	£63.80
£10,000	£66.38	£22.99	£43.40
£20,000	£81.69	£63.80	£17.89
£30,000	£104.62	£104.62	£0.00
£40,000	£119.07	£119.07	£0.00
£50,000	£119,07	£119.07	£0.00

Assumptions: Assumes 49 years in state additional pension scheme.

defined as the average over the last three years before the pension starts of your earnings between the lower and upper earnings limits.

- A pension for your widow or widower if you die first either before or after age 65. The pension must be at least half your pension.

These are minimum terms, so your employer's scheme can provide a better deal – for example, a 1/60th pension, a more generous definition or earnings and a tax-free lump sum at retirement (either in addition to the 1/80th pension or by swapping part for the lump sum)

Although not guaranteed in any way, in practice, most contracted-out final salary schemes are likely to produce a pension as good as the state pension you give up - see table overleaf.

However, if inflation were to run at high levels, you could lose out because, under the state scheme you get full inflation-proofing, whereas salary-related occupational schemes are required only to increase pensions in line with inflation up to a maximum of 2.5 per cent a year (see page 82).

Contracting-out through a salary-related scheme worked differently before 1997. You built up 'guaranteed minimum pension' (GMP) which although not identical to the SERPS given up was based on it and generally a fair substitute. Before 1997, if your GMPs fell short of the SERPS given up, the state topped up your pension so you could not lose by contracting out.

Contracting out through a money purchase scheme

In a contracted-out money purchase scheme, your employer is required to invest an amount in the occupational scheme equal to the National

Jargon buster

Reference scheme A notional pension scheme with pension and other benefits that set the minima which a contracted-out salary-related scheme must match.

Planning point

If you contract out through a salary-related occupational scheme, the pension you'll get is likely to be as good as or better than the state additional pension you give up.

Insurance you have both saved. (Your employer may require you to meet some of this cost by paying contributions to the scheme.) The fund which builds up must be used to provide the following 'protected rights':

- A pension for you payable from any age from 50 onwards (increasing to 55 by 2010). This can be provided through an annuity or income withdrawal (see Chapter 5). You must be allowed to shop around and choose your own annuity if you want to and annuity rates must be unisex (in other words the same, regardless of your gender).
- If you are married at the time you start your pension, a pension for your widow/er or civil partner equal to at least half your pension.
- A pension for your widow/er or civil partner if you die before retirement

Contracted-out salary-related scheme vs S2P given up

Earnings	S2P given up	Contracted-out pension built up in reference scheme
£5,000	£2.58	£7.90
£10,000	£22.99	£70.40
£20,000	£63.80	£195.40
£30,000	£104.62	£320.40
£40,000	£119.07	£364.65
£50,000	£119.07	£364.65

(equal to whatever amount the fund will buy).

- Since April 2006, if you choose, a tax-free lump sum up to a quarter of the value of the fund.

Since 6 April 2005, there is no requirement for pensions to be increased once they start to be paid. It is up to you to decide whether you want some built-in increases, say, to protect your income against rising prices (see Chapter 5).

When you contract out on a money purchase basis, as with any money purchase scheme, you cannot know in advance how much pension you will get. It depends on:

- The amount paid in.
- How well the invested contributions grow.

- The charges deducted.
- Annuity rates at the time you want to start the pension.

Therefore, it is impossible to say with certainty whether or not you will be better off or worse off by contracting out. All you can do is make estimates based on assumptions which may turn out to be wrong or right. However, one factor is known: the minimum amount that must be paid into the scheme.

The table below gives examples of the total that must be paid into the scheme in 2006-7 depending on your age and earnings. The amount tends to increase with age because as well as the National Insurance saving an extra sum is paid in, which is age-related to reflect the increasing cost of providing pensions for people getting closer to retirement.

Minimum annual amounts that must be paid into a contracted-out money purchase scheme (2006-7)

	Age at end of previous tax year and percentage of earnings between lower and upper earnings limits that must be invested				
Your earnings	20 2.8%	30 3.4%	40 4.2%	50 5.9%	60 9.9%
£5,000	£18	£21	£27	£37	£63
£10,000	£158	£191	£237	£332	£558
£20,000	£438	£531	£657	£922	£1,548
£30,000	£718	£871	£1,077	£1,512	£2,538
£40,000	£817	£992	£1,225	£1,721	£2,888
£50,000	£817	£992	£1,225	£1,721	£2,888

POSSIBLE PENSION IF YOU CONTRACT OUT THROUGH A MONEY PURCHASE SCHEME

The charts show how much pension in today's money the contracted-out scheme might provide by age 65 compared with the estimated S2P given up, depending on age and the amount earnt. The charts assume investments grow at either 3 or 1 per cent a year more than the rate of inflation; scheme charges are 1 per cent a year; and you use the pension fund to buy an RPI-linked annuity for a couple with a 50 per cent widow/er's pension. The charts

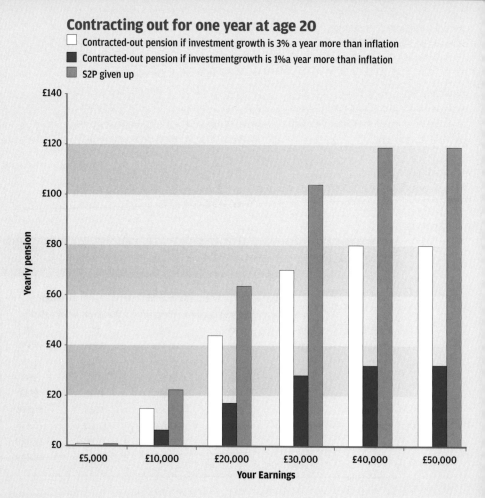

Contracting out for one year at age 20

☐ Contracted-out pension if investment growth is 3% a year more than inflation

■ Contracted-out pension if investmentgrowth is 1%a year more than inflation

■ S2P given up

suggest that contracting out is unlikely to be worthwhile, especially at older ages. Yet it could be worthwhile using more optimistic assumptions. Consider the whole package of benefits offered by your occupational scheme before deciding whether the gain from contracting back in would outweigh the benefits you give up by leaving the scheme.

> **!** **Contracting-out alert**
> Have you contracted out of SERPS or S2P into a personal pension? If your adviser didn't make it clear that the policy could provide a lower pension than the state and didn't check that you understood this risk, you may have been mis-sold.

Contracting out for one year at age 40

□ Contracted-out pension if investment growth is 3% a year more than inflation
■ Contracted-out pension if investmentgrowth is 1%a year more than inflation
▩ S2P given up

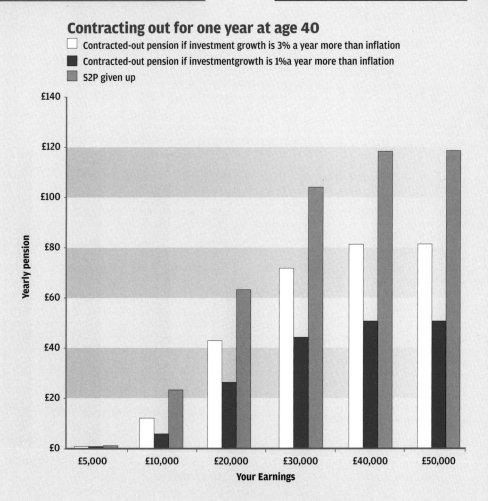

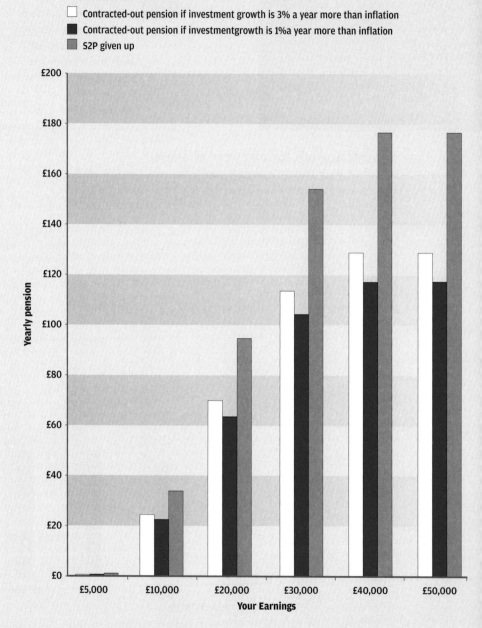

Contracting out for one year at age 60

☐ Contracted-out pension if investment growth is 3% a year more than inflation
■ Contracted-out pension if investmentgrowth is 1%a year more than inflation
▨ S2P given up

Yearly pension (y-axis): £0, £20, £40, £60, £80, £100, £120, £140, £160, £180, £200

Your Earnings (x-axis): £5,000, £10,000, £20,000, £30,000, £40,000, £50,000

CONTRACTING OUT THROUGH A PERSONAL PENSION

If you belong to an occupational scheme which is not contracted out or do not belong to any occupational scheme, you can decide whether or not to contract out.

In this case, you contract out by taking out a personal pension, which can be a stakeholder scheme. There are restrictions on the use of self-invested personal pensions (SIPPS) for contracting out.

Technically, you can also contract out using a free-standing AVC scheme. In practice, this route does not offer such a good deal and has been little used.

National Insurance Rebate

When you contract out through a personal pension, you and your employer carry on paying National Insurance at the normal rates. But part of the contributions is refunded direct to your contracted-out scheme. This refund is called the 'NI rebate'.

Giving up S2P

The NI rebate is set to reflect the amount of S2P you are giving up.

Most people give up their whole S2P for any year in which they are contracted-out. The exception is where you earn less than the low earnings threshold (£12,500 in 2006-7). In this case, to work out your S2P, you are treated as if you have earnings equal to the threshold. But the rebate is worked out as a percentage of your actual earnings. This means the rebate is smaller than the amount needed to compensate you fully for the loss of your whole S2P. To cope with this mismatch, you give up only part of your S2P in line with your actual earnings and still get the rest from the state as usual – see below.

Estimated S2P given up when contracting out through a personal pension (2006-7)

Your earnings £ a year	S2P for year if you are in the state scheme £ a year	S2P given up if you contract out £ a year	Residual S2P you still get if contracted out £ a year
£5,000	£66.38	£5.16	£61.22
£10,000	£66.38	£45.98	£20.41
£20,000	£81.69	£81.69	£0.00
£30,000	£104.62	£104.62	£0.00
£40,000	£119.07	£119.07	£0.00
£50,000	£119.07	£119.07	£0.00

Assumptions: Assumes 49 years in state additional pension scheme.

Pension from the contracted-out personal scheme

The rebates must be used to provide the same 'protected rights' that apply to money purchase occupational schemes (see page 128). As with any money purchase pension, you cannot know in advance how much pension you will get. It depends on:

- The amount paid in.
- How well your invested fund grows.
- The charges deducted.
- Annuity rates at the time you start your pension.

The amount paid in is the rebate set by the government. In addition, you get tax relief on the part of the rebate that is a refund of your (rather than your employer's) National Insurance. The tax relief is also paid into your scheme. The table below gives some examples of the rebates for 2006-7 including tax relief, depending on your age and earnings. The amount increases with age reflecting the higher cost of providing a pension for someone who is closer to retirement than for a younger person.

The personal pension rebates are in most cases higher than the equivalent sums paid to money purchase occupational schemes. But the amount of S2P given up at lower levels of earnings is greater. The overall outcome is similar to but slightly more promising than that shown in the charts on pages 130–2:

- If investment performance averages 3 per cent a year more than inflation, charges average 1 per cent a year and annuity rates do not deteriorate, you might get a higher pension by contracting out.
- But if investments grow by just 1 per cent a year more than inflation, the contracted-out pension falls short of the state pension given up.

NI rebates for contracted-out personal pensions (2006-7)

Your earnings	Age at end of previous tax year				
	20	30	40	50	60
£5,000	£58	£64	£70	£89	£133
£10,000	£521	£566	£622	£791	£1,186
£20,000	£958	£1,038	£1,139	£1,442	£2,147
£30,000	£1,243	£1,346	£1,474	£1,859	£2,756
£40,000	£1,415	£1,532	£1,678	£2,115	£3,136
£50,000	£1,415	£1,532	£1,678	£2,115	£3,136

CONTRACTING OUT ON A MONEY PURCHASE BASIS – PROS AND CONS

Deciding whether or not to contract out on a money purchase basis is tricky. You are swapping what is in effect a salary-related pension (the state additional pension) for the uncertainties of money purchase.

The state additional pension scheme has been changed many times since it started in 1978 – usually for the worse – and there is no guarantee that there will be no further changes. On the other hand, you have all the usual risks of money purchase, in particular:

- Investment risk. If your investments perform badly, you could end up with a much lower pension than the state pension you gave up. If they perform well, you could get a higher pension.
- People living longer. If life expectancy continues to rise, it is possible that annuity rates will fall further, which means that at any given age you

would be able to buy less pension with the fund that had built up.

If you are not comfortable with risk, you may be better off staying in the state scheme.

> ❝ You are swapping what is, in effect, a salary-related pension for the uncertainties of money purchase. ❞

Assuming you don't mind taking some risk, you need to decide how likely it is that the amount your employer or the government pays into your scheme will succeed in providing a better pension than the S2P you give up. Some points to consider include:

- The rebates generally increase with age but have been capped from about age 55 or so onwards. Therefore, if your age is beyond mid-50s, contracting out may be a poor deal.
- The rebates are set on the assumption that, at retirement, you will be married and have to buy a pension that allows for a pension for your widow/er. If you are not married, you can opt for a single-life annuity which will give you a higher income. This makes it more likely that you can gain from contracting out.

Another point in favour of contracting out is that contracted-out schemes are more flexible than the state scheme.

Planning point

When thinking about contracting out through a personal pension, you cannot make a decision with any certainty. All you can do is base your decision on reasonable assumptions with which you feel comfortable. You will not know until you start to draw your pension whether your decision was a good or bad one.

Case Study Jenny

Jenny is 20 and earns £20,000 a year. If she contracts out through a personal pension in 2006-7, she will be giving up roughly £82 a year of eventual state pension (see table, page 133). In return, the government will pay an NI rebate plus tax relief of £958 into her personal pension (see page 134). Based on current annuity rates, this might provide a pension in today's money of, say, £89 a year if the invested rebate grows by an average 3 per cent a year more than inflation. But if investment growth averaged only 1 per cent a year more than inflation, the pension would be only £38 a year – a lot less than the estimated S2P given up. Jenny has no way of knowing how the future will turn out but she's not keen on too much risk and decides to stay in the state scheme.

You can take your pension at any age from 50 onwards (rising to 55 from 2010) but must wait until state pension age to draw the state pension. Also, since 6 April 2006, you can – provided the scheme rules allow – take a quarter of the contracted-out personal pension fund as a tax-free lump sum; the state provides pensions only at state pension age.

GETTING ADVICE

If you are unsure about your contracted-out status or the options open to you, get in touch with the pensions administrator at work. They will not be able to advise you on the decision to contract out or not through a personal pension. But they may be able to put you in touch with an independent financial adviser (IFA) who can help – this is particularly likely if there are already arrangements to take out a group personal pension or stakeholder scheme through your workplace.

If your workplace can't help, you can get in touch with either a pension provider if you have already chosen the particular personal pension you want to use or an IFA. However, IFAs generally prefer to deal only with reasonably wealthy clients and may be reluctant to give you advice if the amount of pension involved is small.

KEEPING TRACK

You should receive a yearly benefit statement from your contracted-out scheme showing, in today's money, the pension you might get by your specified pension age. Any state pension forecast will take into account periods for which you have been contracted out.

Free leaflets about contracting out

Reference	Title	From
CA17	Employee's guide to the minimum contributions	HM Revenue & Customs
PM7	Contracted-out pensions – your guide	The Pension Service
CRED7bP	Contracting out of the the state second pension	Financial Services Authority

Leaving a scheme early

Leaving a pension scheme before you retire creates choices. In some cases you can get a refund of your contributions but normally you will have to choose between leaving your money invested or arranging to transfer it to a new scheme. The best option depends on several factors and needs careful consideration.

Leaving a scheme before retirement

Whatever your reason for quitting, you face a range of options if you leave a pension scheme before retirement. Should you leave your money where it is or is it better to arrange a transfer? These are complicated choices and you may want to get professional advice before reaching a final decision.

There are various reasons why you might leave a pension scheme before retirement. You might decide to leave an occupational scheme on, for example, changing jobs or being made redundant. (You might have to leave if the scheme is being wound up – in that case, see Chapter 10.) You might leave a personal pension because an alternative scheme seems to offer a better deal or greater choice.

Whatever the reason, you face a range of options. They are complicated choices and you may want to get professional advice. You will have some or all of these options:

- Cancel your pension rights and take a refund of contributions.
- Leave your pension rights where they are in the old scheme.
- Transfer your rights to a new scheme.

REFUND OF YOUR CONTRIBUTIONS

Getting a refund is an option only if:
- You are leaving an occupational pension scheme.

Right to transfer

If you have been in an occupational scheme less than two years but at least three months, whatever other options the scheme offers, it must let you transfer the pension rights you have built up to another pension scheme. See page 142 for information about transfers.

- You have been in the pension scheme less than two years.
- The scheme rules allow refunds.

You can have a refund only of your own contributions, not any made on your behalf by your employer. Tax will have been deducted at a rate of 20 per cent on the first £10,800 (in 2006-7) and 40 per cent on anything above that. You cannot reclaim any of this tax but neither is there further tax to pay.

The scheme might add interest to the refund. This is treated separately from the refund and paid with tax at the savings rate (20 per cent in 2006-7) already deducted. If you are a non-taxpayer or starting-rate taxpayer, you can reclaim all or part of the tax. If you are a higher-rate taxpayer, there is extra tax to pay.

If, through being a member of the scheme, you have been contracted-out of the state additional pension (see Chapter 6) and the scheme was salary-related, there will also be a deduction from your refund to cover the cost of buying you back into the state second pension (The period of contracting out is then cancelled and your state pension reinstated.)

Case Study | Elspeth

Elspeth is changing jobs. She has been in her employer's occupational scheme for 18 months. The scheme tells her she can either have a refund of her contributions or, if she prefers, transfer her pension rights to a new scheme of her choice. The refund being offered is £1,350 (18 months' worth of contributions at 5 per cent of Elspeth's earnings of £18,000 a year without any interest) less tax at 20 per cent of £270, giving a net refund of £1,080.

❝ Taking a refund means losing all the contributions made on your behalf by your employer. ❞

If you have been contracted out through a money purchase occupational scheme, you cannot be reinstated in the state scheme and you can't have a refund in respect of any of these contracted-out pension rights. They must either be left in the old scheme or transferred to a new one.

LEAVING PENSION RIGHTS IN THE OLD SCHEME

If you leave an occupational scheme before retirement but after being a member for at least two years, you must be allowed to leave your pension rights behind so you still get a pension from the scheme later on. (Some occupational schemes also offer this option to members of less than two years.) Similarly, if you have a personal pension, you can stop paying in but leave your savings in the scheme to provide a pension later on. Whatever the type of scheme, this eventual 'preserved pension' will be lower than if you had not left.

To keep track of how much a 'preserved' occupational pension might pay out, the scheme will provide you with regular benefit statements - see page 98.

139

Preserved pension: salary-related scheme

When you leave a salary-related scheme, your eventual pension is worked out in two steps:

- First, calculate the pension according to the normal formula that we looked at in Chapter 4: **Years in scheme** x **Accrual rate** x **Salary = Pension**.
- Then, increase the formula pension, generally, in line with price inflation up to a maximum of 5 per cent a year on average over the period from when you left the scheme up to the date when you start to draw your pension.

This will produce a lower pension than had you not left, firstly, because you have spent fewer years in the scheme. Secondly, 'salary' means your pay calculated at the time you leave the scheme not at retirement. So you lose the effect of any career progression – this could be particularly important if you belong to a final salary scheme. Thirdly, although preserved pensions are increased up to the time they start, the increase is in line only with price inflation and up to a maximum limit. Had you stayed, your pension – by being linked to your pay - would have tended to keep pace with general earnings inflation and there is no 5 per cent a year cap. So losing the earnings link reduces your pension.

Case Study Sayed

Sayed, 40, currently earns £40,000 and has been in a final salary scheme for the last 15 years. It promises one-sixtieth of final salary for each year of membership. If he stays on until retirement at 65, with promotion he expects his pay then to be about £60,000 in today's money. His 15 years' membership so far would be worth 15 x 1/60 x £60,000 = £15,000 a year in pension. But Sayed is changing job. If he leaves the scheme now, his pension will be just 15 x 1/60 x £40,000 = £10,000 and this will be increased in line with prices (not earnings) up to age 65. Sayed needs to ensure the pay package in his new job adequately compensates for the reduction in pension from his old job.

Preserved pension: money purchase scheme

When you leave a money purchase scheme (whether an occupation scheme or personal pension), the pension fund you have built up so far is left invested to continue growing. The pension you eventually get will be lower than had you not left because:

- Future contributions cease. With an occupational scheme, this means losing the future contributions your employer would have paid in on your behalf.
- With a personal pension (other than a stakeholder scheme – see page 102), there might be extra charges if you stop paying in and had previously agreed to make regular contributions.

Preserved pension: contracted-out scheme

Contracted-out pension rights are treated the same as above, except where you are leaving a contracted-out salary-related scheme and had built up rights before April 1997. As described in Chapter 6, in that case, you are entitled to a guaranteed

Jargon buster

Preserved pension The pension you are promised at normal pension age from a scheme you have left.

minimum pension (GMP) broadly equivalent to the state additional pension given up. If you leave before normal pension age, this GMP must be increased between the time you leave and state pension age by either:

- The increase in national average earnings. This method tends to produce the best increases, but in practice is used only by public sector schemes, or
- A fixed percentage, regardless of actual price or earnings inflation. For people leaving in early 2006, the fixed rate was 4.5 per cent a year (unchanged since 2002).

Bear in mind that the state tops up the increased GMPs through your remaining state additional pension to ensure that you get no less pension overall than you would have done had you not contracted out.

Planning point

In general, be wary of transferring from a salary-related pension scheme to a money purchase scheme. You are giving up a promised level of pension and getting instead benefits whose value will depend on investment returns and annuity rates – in other words, you will be taking on extra risks (see Chapter 4).

TRANSFERRING YOUR PENSION RIGHTS

Instead of leaving pension rights in an old scheme, you may be able to transfer them to a new one, but you need to check:

- The rules of the old scheme allow transfers – most do.
- Whether the new scheme is willing to accept the transfer. It doesn't have to and in some cases may not be able to – for example, if you are transferring contracted-out rights but the new scheme is not contracted out.

You don't have to transfer at the time you leave – you can do it at any time provided you haven't started to draw the benefits. Whether or not to transfer

Jargon buster

Section 32 scheme A pension scheme offered by insurance companies. It is designed to accept preserved pension rights from an occupational scheme and can maintain them in their original form (say, salary-related).

is one of the most difficult pension decisions you'll have to make. The benefits from the new scheme will be different from the benefits you give up in the old scheme, making comparison tricky. The decision is especially difficult where you are exchanging a salary-related for a money purchase pension or vice versa. The table below summarises when this will be the case.

Transferring your pension

Transferring your pension may involve moving from a salary-related scheme to a money purchase scheme. You should be aware of what this implies in terms of risk before deciding to move. See Planning point page 141.

Scheme you are transferring out of	Scheme you are transferring into			
	Occupational salary-related	Occupational money purchase	Section 32	Personal pension (inc. stakeholder scheme)
Occupational salary-related	SR–SR	SR–MP	SR–SR	SR–MP
Occupational money purchase	MP–SR	MP–MP	MP–MP	MP–MP
Personal pension (inc. stakeholder scheme)	MP–SR	MP–MP	Not applicable	MP–MP

SR = salary-related; MP = money purchase.

PROS AND CONS OF PENSION TRANSFERS

It's not easy to decide whether or not you will benefit from transferring your pension. You need to weigh up a range of factors.

PROS

1. Convenience. It is easier to keep track of just one scheme rather than several and easier to draw a pension from just one.

2. Better deal. You might reckon the new scheme is likely to produce a higher pension than the old one.

3. Future benefit improvements. A scheme might include transferred rights in any improvements to the scheme, but probably not preserved pension rights.

4. Economies of scale. With personal pensions, charges may be lower for bigger funds.

5. Greater choice. A new scheme might offer, say, a wider range of investments.

6. Sever contact with a former employer - for example, if you parted on bad terms.

7. Fears about the employer's solvency. If your former employer's business fails, there is some risk that any salary-related pension scheme might be left short of enough funds to meet its pension promises (but see Chapter 10).

CONS

1. Loss of guaranteed benefits. Some money purchase schemes offer guaranteed annuity rates when you start your pension. Because annuity rates have fallen sharply in recent years, these rates are now hard to beat.

2. Reduced pension from salary-related schemes. Because each scheme uses different assumptions, the benefits you are promised in the new scheme may well be lower than the benefits you are giving up (but see page 148).

3. Extra charges. The scheme you leave may deduct a surrender charge - most likely with personal pensions (other than stakeholder schemes) and some money purchase occupational schemes. If you switch from an occupational scheme to a personal pension, the charges you bear will almost certainly increase.

4. Extra risk. Consolidating your pensions in one scheme means putting all your eggs in one basket. Transferring from a salary-related to a money purchase scheme, means you taking on extra risk.

HOW TRANSFERS WORK

When a pension transfer takes place, the old scheme pays a cash sum to the new scheme. The big questions are: how much cash will the old scheme pay and what benefits will that sum buy in the new scheme? The answers depend on the types of scheme involved.

Jargon buster

Transfer value The lump sum which, if invested now, is deemed to be enough to provide a given level of pension at retirement plus other benefits. This cash sum can be transferred from one scheme to another.

Actuary Financial and statistical expert who uses mathematical techniques to estimate how the future may turn out. With pension schemes, actuaries design schemes and advise on issues, such as, the expected size of future benefits and level of contributions needed to ensure those benefits can be paid.

Transferring from a salary-related scheme

A salary-related scheme generally promises a given level of pension, tax-free lump sum, dependants' pensions if you die, and so on. A value – called the 'cash equivalent transfer value' (CETV) or just 'transfer value' - has to be put on these benefits to arrive at the cash sum the old scheme is willing to pay if you give them up.

Calculating the transfer value is complex and carried out by the scheme's actuary. However, the broad steps are:

- Work out your preserved pension at the time you leave the scheme.
- Increase the pension between now and the normal pension age for the scheme as described on pages 140-1.
- Work out the lump sum that would be required at retirement to buy that pension based on assumptions about annuity rates, dependant's pension and pension increases in retirement.
- Work out the amount of cash you would need to invest today to produce the required lump sum at retirement based on assumptions about investment returns and the sort of investments the pension scheme would be invested in.
- Similarly, work out the value of other benefits, based on appropriate assumptions (for example, the probability of dying at any given age). However, the actuary does not necessarily take into account benefits that are 'discretionary', in other words, not promised but paid only if the trustees decide to.
- The resulting transfer value can be reduced – but not below a minimum level worked out on a statutory basis – if the pension fund does not have enough in it to meet all the members' promised benefits in full.

As you can see, the actuary has to make a number of assumptions. Even quite small changes in the assumptions can have a big impact on the resulting transfer value. Although there are standard professional guidelines and the statutory minimum basis for the calculation, the actuary has a lot of discretion to choose assumptions that are relevant to the particular scheme.

The assumptions depend also on economic conditions at the time, so any transfer value quoted is valid for a maximum of three months. If you don't make your decision within that time, you need to ask the scheme for a new quote. If conditions have changed the new quote may give a higher or lower transfer value.

Transferring from a money purchase scheme

The transfer value from a money purchase scheme (whether an occupational scheme or a personal pension) is simply the value of the pension fund earmarked for you, less any surrender charges.

The value of the pension fund of course depends on the value of the past contributions paid in by your employer and, if it is a contributory scheme, you as well, together with past investment income and growth. The value of the fund rises and falls with stock market conditions, so the transfer value only becomes a fixed precise amount at the date of transfer.

Case Study | Sayed

Sayed is leaving a final salary scheme at age 40 and is entitled to a preserved pension of £10,000 a year payable from age 65. For simplicity, assume there are no other benefits and that the pension once it starts will be increased in line with price inflation. Instead of the preserved pension, Sayed wants to transfer to a new scheme. The old scheme's actuary works out the transfer value as follows:

• The preserved pension is £10,000 a year payable in 25 years' time
• Assuming inflation averages 2.5 per cent a year, the revalued preserved pension would be £18,500 by age 65
• Using an RPI-linked annuity rate for a single man aged 65, the actuary works out that a lump sum of £396,000 would be needed at age 65 to provide a pension of £18,500
• Assuming investment returns average 8.5 per cent a year and scheme costs 0.75 per cent a year, £61,000 would need to be invested today to generate the required lump sum by age 65.

Therefore, Sayed's transfer value is £61,000.

Transferring to a salary-related scheme

When you approach a salary-related scheme with a transfer value to pay in, you may be able to use it in one or a choice of the following ways:

- Buy a fixed amount of pension payable at the normal pension age for the scheme. This is basically a preserved pension but it is unlikely to be the same as the amount of preserved pension you have given up in the old scheme – see below.
- Buy 'added years' in the new scheme. This means that when your pension and other benefits are worked out, a higher number of years are included in the formula than your actual years of membership. This results in a higher pension and other benefits. The number of years in the new scheme that you can buy may be fewer than the number of years you had in the old scheme – see below.
- Invest on a money purchase basis and eventually use the resulting fund to buy extra pension or other benefits. This is generally the least desirable option if you are transferring from a salary-related scheme because you will be taking on extra risk compared with the salary-related preserved pension you have given up in the old scheme.

To convert your transfer value into a fixed pension or added years, the actuary of the new scheme has basically to reverse the steps of the old scheme's actuary described on page 144. This means working out how much the transfer value, if invested now, could be worth by the normal pension age for the scheme, then calculating how much pension that fund could provide, based once again on various assumptions.

The calculations by the actuaries in the old and new schemes are similar but the assumptions they use are likely to differ. The benefits which make up the package from each scheme will also differ. The upshot is that what you can buy in the new scheme is very unlikely to be identical to the benefits you give up in the old scheme. It can seem very confusing but, just because the pension or number of added years in the new scheme is lower than that from the old scheme, it does not necessarily mean you are being offered an inferior deal.

TRANSFER CHECKLIST

These are the main factors to consider before deciding whether or not to transfer from one scheme to another.

1. GUARANTEED BENEFITS
If the old scheme offers guaranteed benefits – for example, a retirement annuity contract with a guaranteed annuity rate – be wary of any transfer that means giving up the guarantee.

2. TRANSFER CLUB
If both schemes are in a transfer club (see page 148), transferring is likely to be worthwhile.

3. EXPECTED PENSION
Compare the benefits from the old scheme with what you might get from the new scheme. Get help making the comparison (see page 150).

4. RISK
Before choosing a money purchase scheme over a salary-related one, make sure you understand and are comfortable with the extra risks (see Chapter 4).

5. WHEN YOU CAN START YOUR PENSION
Check the normal pension age and early/late retirement options for both schemes Are you happy with the options?

6. DEATH BENEFITS
If you have dependants, check out the life cover and dependants' pensions. If you are not married or registered to your partner, check they are eligible for a dependant's pension under the scheme rules – see Chapter 8.

7. RETIRING EARLY THROUGH ILL HEALTH
Check the pension that would be payable from each scheme in this event.

8. OTHER BENEFITS
Does the old scheme offer any extras to members with preserved pensions and/or to its pensioners? For example, medical insurance, discounts on the employer's products, membership of a pensioners' club, use of company sports facilities? Does the new scheme offer anything similar?

Transferring to a money purchase scheme

Transfers into money purchase schemes are very straightforward. Your transfer value is a cash sum which is invested in the pension fund and earmarked to buy your pension and other benefits in the normal way. As with all money purchase schemes, your eventual pension will depend on:

- The amount paid in.
- How well the invested transfer value grows.
- Charges deducted.
- Annuity rates at the time you want to start the pension.

Transfer clubs

A transfer club is an arrangement between different salary-related pension schemes to pay transfers out and accept transfers in using the same or similar assumptions. This means, you should be treated more or less as if you had been a continuous member of one scheme for the whole time you spent in the various schemes in the club.

The biggest of these clubs is the Public Sector Transfer Club which links many public sector schemes (covering, for example, the armed forces, teachers, universities, police, the NHS, and so on) and some other schemes mainly for charitable and similar bodies. The schemes you are leaving and joining can tell you if they are both members of a transfer club.

Planning point

Each time you leave a salary-related scheme early, you suffer the drawbacks described on page 140. So anyone who changes jobs often should generally be wary of transferring their pension from one salary-related scheme to another unless they can take advantage of a transfer club - see below left.

Transferring contracted-out pension rights

If you have been contracted-out of the state additional scheme (see Chapter 6) through the pension scheme you are leaving, there are special rules and points to consider when transferring your contracted-out pension rights – see the table, right.

Contracted-out rights can only be transferred to another contracted-out scheme. This might be a contracted-out occupational scheme or a contracted-out personal pension (including a stakeholder scheme).

Except where a pension scheme is wound up with a deficit (see Chapter 10), there is no option to transfer back into the state additional pension scheme.

Contracted-out transfers

Type of transfer	Points to consider
From a salary-related to a salary-related scheme	Your preserved pension is made up of guaranteed minimum pension (GMP) and/or reference scheme benefits (see pages 127-8). Either way, these are promised levels of pensions. There are only two transfers that keep the pension promise: transfer to a new employer's contracted-out salary-related occupational scheme or to a section 32 scheme. However, the insurance companies that offer section 32 schemes are reluctant to accept GMP transfers because the benefits are costly to replicate.
From a salary-related scheme to a money purchase (personal pension or occupational scheme)	You lose the pension promise and instead get protected rights (see page 128).
From a salary-related scheme providing reference scheme benefits (see page 127)	Even if the scheme provides better pensions and other benefits than the minimum required, the whole of your transfer value counts as a transfer of contracted-out rights. So, for example, if you were transferring to a personal pension, the whole transfer value would have to buy protected rights.
From a money purchase to a salary-related scheme	This type of transfer is possible in theory, but in practice the new scheme might decline the transfer because it is likely to be too small to pay for the typically more costly salary-related benefits.
From a money purchase to a money purchase scheme	Both the old and new schemes must provide protected rights (see page 128).

149

GETTING INFORMATION AND ADVICE

If you are leaving or joining an occupational scheme, the pension scheme administrator can give you information about the scheme, your scheme benefits and the options you face, but they are unlikely to be able to give you advice. Your employer might recommend an independent financial adviser (IFA) and might be willing to pay towards the advice. (Pensions advice costing more than £150 a year paid for by your employer normally counts as a taxable benefit from your job.)

To find your own IFA use, for example, a search tool such as www.unbiased.co.uk. To advise on pension transfers, an adviser must be a specialist holding extra qualifications. You can check that an IFA is allowed to give transfer advice using the FSA Register at www.fsa.gov.uk/register. You can pay for an IFA's advice by fee – say, £75 to £250 an hour. You might agree instead for the adviser to be paid by commission from the provider of any product you take up (in which case you pay indirectly through the product charges).

Where you are transferring from a scheme that provides promised or guaranteed benefits to a personal pension or other money purchase scheme, the IFA must carry out a 'transfer value analysis'. This works out the investment return (the 'critical yield') you would need from the money purchase scheme to produce a pension that matched the one you are giving up. It's impossible to say what return you will actually get – a typical assumption might be 5 or 7 per cent a year. The higher the critical yield, the more likely you are to lose out by transferring.

You could consider advice from a consulting actuary but this is costly and appropriate only if you have a large sum to transfer.

Planning point

Over a million people received redress amounting to over £10 billion after being wrongly advised in the late-1980s/early-1990s to transfer from occupational schemes to personal pensions, losing valuable benefits in the process.
Make sure you understand what you are giving up if you transfer out of an occupational scheme.

Pensions and your family

Pension schemes are primarily designed to provide retirement income but they are also an important source of bereavement benefits. Many occupational and personal schemes offer lump-sum pay outs for your survivors, as well as an on-going income. As a valuable asset, pension savings are also an important consideration in divorce proceedings.

Pensions and dependants

The main purpose of pension schemes is to provide retirement income, but they also provide death benefits and so are important in planning for your family's security. Pensions are also key assets to be taken into account when families split up.

STATE PENSIONS AND BENEFITS ON DEATH

The state provides specific help for widows, widowers and bereaved civil partners but not for unmarried or unregistered partners. The rules are complicated and an outline is given here – see the table on page 154 for sources of further information.

Death before retirement

If you die before your spouse or civil partner has reached state pension age, they may be able to claim the following state bereavement benefits if you had built up the appropriate National Insurance record over your working life up to the time of your death:

- **Bereavement payment.** This is a tax-free lump sum of £2,000.
- **Widowed parent's allowance.** A regular taxable income set at the same level as the state basic pension (£84.25 a week in 2006-7) plus half (or sometimes more) of any state additional pension (S2P) you had built up – see Box right. The payment continues until the youngest child ceases to be dependent or until your widow, widower or civil partner, enters a new marriage or civil partnership or starts to live with someone as if they were married or registered. There is no extra amount per child (as there used to be in the past), but your spouse or civil partner might also be able to claim child tax credit (a means-tested

❝ Occupational and personal schemes may offer pensions and lump sum pay-outs for your survivors when you die. ❞

To find out more about bereavement benefits contact your local Jobcentre Plus (see your phonebook) if you are of working age or visit their website at www.jobcentreplus.gov.uk

Inherited state pension

If you die your spouse or civil partner inherits half of any state second pension you had built up (see Chapter 2). In addition, they can inherit at least half of any SERPS pension entitlement you had - the amount depends on the date when you reached, or would have reached, state pension age:

- **Before 6 October 2002:** 100 per cent of your SERPS pension

- **6 October 2002 to 5 October 2004:** 90 per cent of your SERPS pension

- **6 October 2004 to 5 October 2006:** 80 per cent

- **6 October 2006 to 5 October 2008:** 70 per cent

- **6 October 2008 to 5 October 2010:** 60 per cent

- **6 October 2010 onwards:** 50 per cent.

But the amount of any inherited SERPS plus any SERPS you have built up in your own right must not exceed the maximum that a single person could have. In 2005-6, the maximum was £143.08 a week.

state benefit available to households with children).

- **Bereavement allowance.** A regular taxable income payable to spouses and civil partners over age 45 without any dependent children. The amount increases with their age – see table on page 154. This income is payable for a maximum of 52 weeks and stops earlier if your spouse or partner enters a new marriage or civil relationship or starts to live with someone as if they were married or registered.

Death after retirement

If you die after you and your spouse or civil partner have both reached state pension age, help is given through the state pension system. Your spouse or partner, if they do not receive a full basic pension in their own right, may be able to make up the pension to the full rate a single person can have (£84.25 a week in 2006-7) by using your contribution record. In addition, they can inherit half (or sometimes more) of any state additional pension you had built up – see the box above.

Planning point

If you have gaps in your National Insurance record, it could be worth paying voluntary Class 3 National Insurance contributions (see page 46) to ensure that your spouse or civil partner would qualify for maximum bereavement benefits in the event of your death - see chart on page 155.

Bereavement allowance (2006-7)

(Payable for a maximum of 52 weeks)

Age of spouse or civil partner when you die	Weekly amount
45	£25.28
46	£31.17
47	£37.07
48	£42.97
49	£48.87
50	£54.76
51	£60.66
£52	£66.56
£53	£72.46
£54	£78.35
55 and over	£84.25

Other state benefits

Although there are no specific state benefits for bereaved unmarried or unregistered partners, they may be able to claim other state benefits. The most important of these are working tax credit if they are in work but on a low income, child tax credit if they have children, pension credit if they are already retired and on a low income, and other means-tested help such as housing benefit and council tax benefit. See the table below for sources of further information. You'll also find online guidance about many benefits on the Jobcentre Plus website www.jobcentreplus.gov.uk. If you don't have access to the internet, see the Address section at the back of this book for alternative contact details.

Free leaflets about state benefits

Reference	Title	From
NP45	A guide to bereavement benefits	Department for Work and Pensions
NP46	A guide to state pensions	The Pension Service
SERPSL1	Important information for married people – inheritance of SERPS	The Pension Service
PC1L	Pension credit	The Pension Service
GL14	Widowed?	Department for Work and Pensions
GL16	Help with your rent	Department for Work and Pensions
GL17	Help with your council tax	Department for Work and Pensions
WTC2	Child tax credit and working tax credit – a guide	HM Revenue & Customs

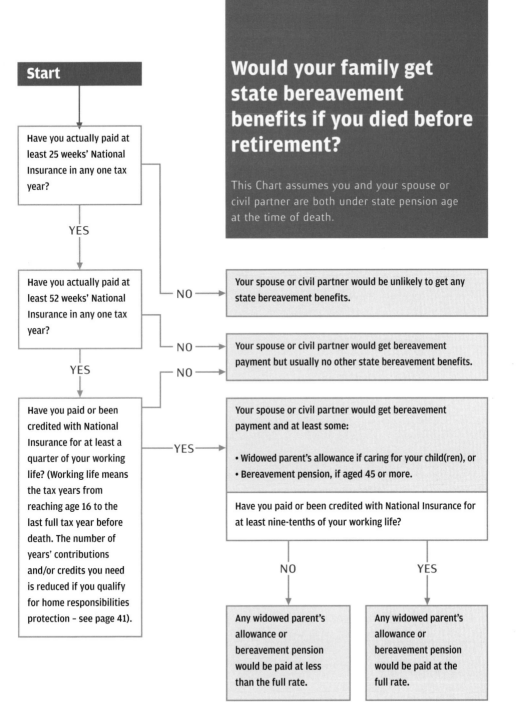

Start

Have you actually paid at least 25 weeks' National Insurance in any one tax year?

YES

Have you actually paid at least 52 weeks' National Insurance in any one tax year?

YES

Have you paid or been credited with National Insurance for at least a quarter of your working life? (Working life means the tax years from reaching age 16 to the last full tax year before death. The number of years' contributions and/or credits you need is reduced if you qualify for home responsibilities protection – see page 41).

Would your family get state bereavement benefits if you died before retirement?

This Chart assumes you and your spouse or civil partner are both under state pension age at the time of death.

— NO → Your spouse or civil partner would be unlikely to get any state bereavement benefits.

— NO → Your spouse or civil partner would get bereavement payment but usually no other state bereavement benefits.

— NO

—YES → Your spouse or civil partner would get bereavement payment and at least some:

• Widowed parent's allowance if caring for your child(ren), or
• Bereavement pension, if aged 45 or more.

Have you paid or been credited with National Insurance for at least nine-tenths of your working life?

NO

YES

Any widowed parent's allowance or bereavement pension would be paid at less than the full rate.

Any widowed parent's allowance or bereavement pension would be paid at the full rate.

DEATH BENEFITS FROM OCCUPATIONAL AND PERSONAL SCHEMES

Occupational and personal schemes may offer pensions and lump sum pay-outs for your survivors when you die. Since April 2006, the tax rules allow greater flexibility than in the past over the amount and type of these benefits and there is no restriction on the proportion of contributions you use to pay for death benefits. But individual schemes can set their own more restrictive rules.

Dependants' pensions – the tax rules

Schemes can pay pensions to your dependants (but not anyone who was not dependent on you) whether you die before or after starting your pension. 'Dependant' means:

- Your husband, wife or civil partner.
- Your child(ren) under the age of 23 or, if older, dependent on you because of physical or mental impairment.
- Anyone else financially dependent on you.
- Anyone financially interdependent with you – for example, an unmarried or unregistered partner with whom you share a home and the associated expenses.
- Anyone dependent on you because of physical or mental impairment.

Planning point

A pension scheme can provide pensions and/or a lump sum for your family if you were to die. This is a tax efficient arrangement because you get tax relief in the normal way on contributions to the scheme, regardless of whether they are buying retirement or death benefits.

All the dependants' pensions added together must not come to more than the retirement pension you would have been entitled to, but otherwise there is no limit on the amount of any one pension.

The pension choices for your dependants are virtually the same as those for a person starting a retirement pension (see Chapters 4 and 5) and are summarised in the Chart opposite. The only difference is that, where a dependant's pension is to be provided by an annuity, no 'guarantee period' (as described on page 112) is allowed.

Dependants' pensions are taxable income, so the recipient will have to pay tax on it if their income from all sources is high enough. Tax is normally deducted through PAYE before the pension is paid out.

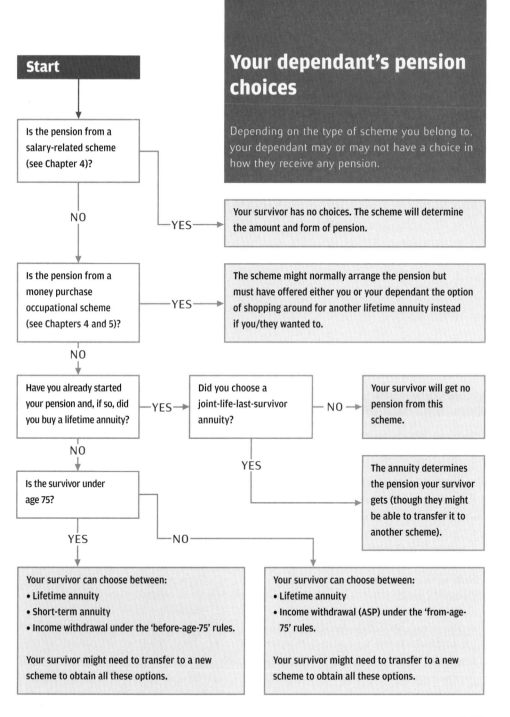

Start

Is the pension from a salary-related scheme (see Chapter 4)?

— NO ↓

— YES → Your survivor has no choices. The scheme will determine the amount and form of pension.

Is the pension from a money purchase occupational scheme (see Chapters 4 and 5)?

— NO ↓

— YES → The scheme might normally arrange the pension but must have offered either you or your dependant the option of shopping around for another lifetime annuity instead if you/they wanted to.

Have you already started your pension and, if so, did you buy a lifetime annuity?

— NO ↓

— YES → Did you choose a joint-life-last-survivor annuity?

— NO → Your survivor will get no pension from this scheme.

— YES ↓

Is the survivor under age 75?

YES ↓   — NO →

The annuity determines the pension your survivor gets (though they might be able to transfer it to another scheme).

YES

Your survivor can choose between:
• Lifetime annuity
• Short-term annuity
• Income withdrawal under the 'before-age-75' rules.

Your survivor might need to transfer to a new scheme to obtain all these options.

NO

Your survivor can choose between:
• Lifetime annuity
• Income withdrawal (ASP) under the 'from-age-75' rules.

Your survivor might need to transfer to a new scheme to obtain all these options.

Your dependant's pension choices

Depending on the type of scheme you belong to, your dependant may or may not have a choice in how they receive any pension.

Dependants' pensions from occupational salary-related schemes

Subject to the tax rules already described, a scheme can set its own rules about how much pension it will provide for dependants. If the scheme is contracted out (see Chapter 6), there are additional rules.

Typically, a scheme will provide a pension for a widow, widower or civil partner on:

● Death before you have started your pension. Pension of, say, half or two-thirds of the pension you would have been entitled to based on your pay now and either your years of membership to date or the number

Case Study   Joan

Joan's husband, Len, had a pension of £14,000 a year from his occupational scheme. When Len died, under the scheme rules, Joan was entitled to a pension of half Len's entitlement but only in respect of the pension he had built up in the last 13 years of his 22 years with the employer (because the scheme had not offered family benefits at all during the earlier years). Instead of getting a widow's pension of around £7,000 a year from the scheme, Joan was told she would get only £4,800 a year.

of years you would have completed had you reached the normal pension age for the scheme.

● Death after you have started your pension. Pension of, say, half or two-thirds of the pension you were getting at the time of death. A higher pension might be payable for, say, the first three or six months following death.

The pension must be increased each year at least in line with inflation up to a maximum of 2.5 per cent a year on average. The rules of the scheme may state that the pension stops if your widow, widower or civil partner remarries or forms a new civil partnership.

Most public sector schemes do not provide a pension for unmarried or unregistered partners. Most private sector schemes do.

Planning points

Most public sector schemes and a few private sector schemes do not provide a dependant's pension for your partner if you were not married or in a civil partnership. If this situation applies to your family, check the rules of your scheme. If there is no pension for your partner, you may want to take out extra life cover. You can buy life cover tax efficiently through, say, a personal pension.

Schemes have often introduced improvements in the past and the latest level of benefits might not apply to your whole membership of the scheme. For example, a dependant's pension of half your pension might be payable in respect of service since a given date with a lower fraction (or no dependant's pension at all) payable in respect of earlier service. You can usually improve the pension from the earlier period by making additional voluntary contributions (see page 93).

If you have been contracted out through a salary-related pension scheme before April 1997, the scheme must pay a guaranteed minimum pension (GMP) to your widow, widower or civil partner equal to half the GMPs you had built up (see page 128). The scheme and state together provide increases which ensure the pension is fully increased each year in line with inflation. If you have been contracted out through a salary-related scheme since April 1997, under the reference scheme rules (see page 127) the scheme must provide a pension for your spouse or civil partner of at least half the pension you would have had.

Most salary-related schemes also provide separate pensions for dependent children.

Dependants' pensions from all types of money purchase scheme

If you die before starting your pension, the pension fund you have built up can be used to provide a dependant's pension. The amount of pension depends on the size of the fund and annuity rates at the time (which determine either the annuity your dependant can buy or the amount of pension they can take through income withdrawal). The

Jargon buster

Single life annuity An investment where you exchange a lump sum (say, your pension fund) for an income payable for as long as you live.

Joint-life-last-survivor annuity An investments where you exchange a lump sum (say, your pension fund) for an income payable until both you and your partner have died. You can choose whether or not the income reduces following the first death.

same applies if you had already started your pension but still had some pension fund left invested (because you were using income withdrawal or short-term annuities).

" A single-life annuity dies with you and your survivor gets no pension at all. "

Where you die after starting your pension and you had opted for a lifetime annuity, what happens depends on whether you had chosen a single-life annuity or a joint-life-last-survivor annuity. A single-life annuity dies with you and your

For more details on contracted out pension schemes see Chapter 6. For details of State second pension (S2P/SERPS), see Chapter 2.

Pensions and your family

Income from a joint-life-last-survivor annuity

	Level annuity	Annuity escalating by 3% a year	RPI-linked annuity
Single-life annuity			
For man aged 65	£720	£504	£468
Joint-life-last-survivor annuity			
For man aged 65, female partner aged 60, income reducing by half if man dies first	£600	£408	£408
For man aged 65, female partner aged 60, income reducing by one third if man dies first	£576	£384	£384
For man aged 65, female partner aged 60, no reduction in income if man dies first	£540	£348	£336

" Money purchase schemes can provide pensions for other dependants, such as children, but these might not be affordable if the pension fund is small. **"**

survivor gets no pension at all. A joint-life-last-survivor annuity carries on paying out after the first of you and your partner dies and continues for as long as the survivor lives. The starting income will be less to reflect the fact that the pension may have to be paid out for longer – see table on page 159. You can choose for the income to continue after the first death either at the same or a reduced rate (say, two-thirds or a half of the full pension).

For more information on annuities see Chapter 5 and in particular page 109 for an explanation of how annuities work.

Case Study | Sonia

Richard retired at age 65 with a pension fund of £80,000. He opted to buy a single-life annuity which provided an income of £80,000 x £720/£10,000 = £5,760 a year. Unfortunately, he died before his partner Sonia and his pension died with him. This left Sonia struggling to make ends meet.

Planning point

The income from a single-life annuity stops on your death and could leave a partner who depends on you financially struggling to manage. Consider a joint-life-last-survivor annuity instead.

In general, annuities can be purchased for any couple regardless of married or registered status, so there is no discrimination against unmarried and unregistered partners. However, in the case of a money purchase occupational scheme, there might (rarely) be a difference in treatment, so check the rules.

If the pension scheme is contracted out, it must provide protected rights (see page 128). This includes a pension for your widow, widower or civil partner (but not an unmarried or unregistered partner)

Case Study | Mysha

Zain also retired at 65 with a pension fund of £80,000. He opted for a joint-life-last-survivor annuity paying a 50 per cent pension if he died before his wife, Mysha. His initial pension was £80,000 x £600/£10,000 = £4,800 a year. When he predeceased Mysha, she continued to receive a yearly pension of £2,400.

of whatever the fund will buy if you die before retirement or half your pension if you die after the pension has started.

In theory, money purchase schemes can provide pensions for other dependants, such as children, but these might not be affordable if the pension fund is relatively small.

Lump sum death benefits – the tax rules

The types of lump sum that can be paid out and how they are treated for tax depends on your age at the time of death and your pension arrangement. They are described below and summarised in the chart on page 165.

If you die before age 75 and before starting your pension, an occupational scheme or personal pension may pay out a tax-free lump sum. This can be paid to anyone – they do not have to be your dependant. The amount paid out is tested against your lifetime allowance (see page 72) and, if it comes to more than your remaining unused allowance, the excess lump sum is taxed at 55 per cent. The standard allowance in 2006-7 is

161

£1.5 million, which means you may be able to arrange up to £1.5 million life cover through your pension scheme(s).

> **" Provided the benefits are within the tax rules described, individual schemes can set their own rules about how much lump sum death benefit they will provide. "**

If you die before age 75 but have already started your pension or an income withdrawal arrangement, the following lump sums might be payable – again to anyone not necessarily a dependant. But, in this case, the lump sum is taxed at a rate of 35 per cent. The possible lump sums are:

- **Pension or annuity with a guarantee period** (see page 112). Typically the guarantee period is five or ten years. If you die within that time, the balance of pension due for the remainder of the period can be rolled up and paid as a lump sum.
- **Annuity protection** (see page 112). An annuity may guarantee to pay out at least as much as its purchase price. If the pension to date comes

to less, the remainder can be paid out on death as a lump sum.
- **Income withdrawal** (see page 114). If you had opted for income withdrawal, the remainder of the pension fund that has not been paid out in pension can be paid out on death as a lump sum.

If you die on or after age 75, you will by then have started your pension or opted for income withdrawal (in the form of an 'alternatively secured pension' – see page 114). If you are getting a pension direct from an occupational scheme or you have bought a lifetime annuity, there will be no lump sum payable on your death. If you are using income withdrawal, some of your pension fund will remain. This cannot be paid out to your heirs as a lump sum and the following restrictions apply to how it can be used:

- If you have dependants (see page 156 for who counts as a dependant), the remaining fund must be used to provide them with a dependant's pension.
- If you have no dependants, the remaining lump sum can either be paid tax-free to a charity that you have nominated or it may be transferred to other members of

For more information on taxes see the HM Revenue & Customs website at www.hmrc.gov.uk or contact your local tax enquiry centre (look in Phone Book under 'HM Revenue & Customs'.

Inheritance tax and death benefit

In general, pensions and lump sums payable on your death from your pension scheme are outside the scope of inheritance tax. However, under the rules from 6 April 2006 onwards, you have a lot of choice about when and how you draw your pension. And it is a fact that, if you decide to start your pension late or draw only a small or no pension, then your heirs are likely to get either a higher dependant's pension and/or lump sum death benefit. In some circumstances, there may be inheritance tax on what you leave.

Where you die before age 75, inheritance tax problem is a problem only where you know your life expectancy is unusually short and you have acted so as to leave a bigger lump sum to your heirs. This could apply, for example, where you are terminally ill but have delayed starting your pension or opted for income withdrawal with a low or no pension.

After age 75, problems arise only if you have opted for an alternatively secured pension. When you die there will be some pension fund left over. If it is used to provide pension for your dependants or goes to charity, there is no inheritance tax. But, if the fund is to go to other members of the pension scheme, inheritance tax applies. The tax is paid by the pension scheme.

your scheme (if any) to be used to provide their eventual pension and other benefits, but see box above.

Provided the benefits are within the tax rules described above, individual schemes can set their own rules about how much lump sum death benefit they will provide.

Lump sums from occupational salary-related schemes

In an occupational salary-related scheme, the tax-free lump sum on death before retirement is usually set as a multiple of your salary (which would be defined as your final salary at the time of death in a final salary scheme or your average salary in a career average scheme). In public sector schemes, the amount is typically two-times your salary. Private sector schemes often set a higher sum, say, four-times salary.

The lump sum death benefit is usually payable to anyone – this is the case, even in schemes that restrict dependants' pensions to married or registered partners. So, normally, an unmarried or unregistered partner can have the lump sum. Usually the scheme will ask you to nominate the person or people you would like to receive it. The scheme does not have to follow your wishes, but generally will do so.

Salary-related schemes do not normally pay out a lump sum on death after you have started your pension.

Lump sums from all types of money purchase schemes

On death before your pension starts, a money purchase scheme typically pays out a lump sum equal to the value of the pension fund that has built up, unless the fund is being used instead to provide a dependant's pension. Alternatively or additionally, some of the contributions to the scheme may have been used to buy life insurance to pay out a lump sum on death. Usually these lump sums are tax-free.

Whether or not a lump sum is payable after the pension has started (and up to age 75) depends on the options you chose. If you bought an annuity with a guarantee period or annuity protection, then a lump sum will be payable if the pension already paid out has not reached the value of the guaranteed sum. If you opted for

❝ The lump sum death benefit is usually payable to anyone. Usually the scheme will ask you to nominate who you would like to receive it. ❞

 If you are in an occupational pension scheme you should have made an 'expression of wish' nominating who is to receive any lump-sum payable if you die before starting to draw pension. If your circumstances have changed, check with the scheme's administrator to make sure that these details are up to date.

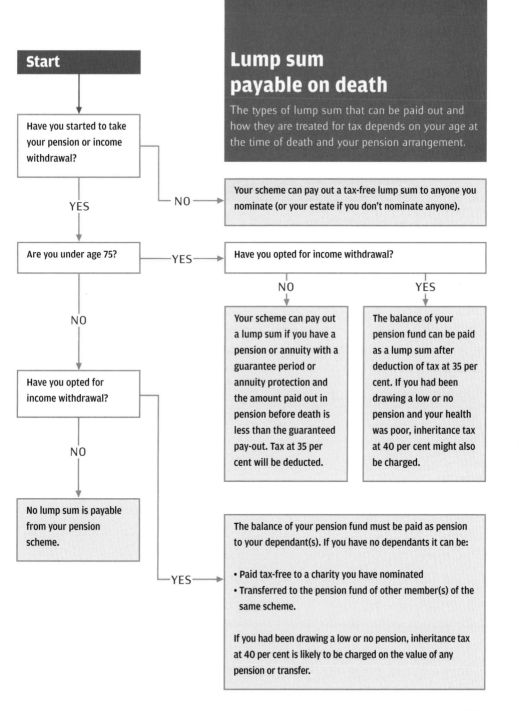

Start

Have you started to take your pension or income withdrawal?

YES ↓ / NO →

Lump sum payable on death

The types of lump sum that can be paid out and how they are treated for tax depends on your age at the time of death and your pension arrangement.

NO → Your scheme can pay out a tax-free lump sum to anyone you nominate (or your estate if you don't nominate anyone).

Are you under age 75?

YES → Have you opted for income withdrawal?

NO ↓

       NO   YES

Your scheme can pay out a lump sum if you have a pension or annuity with a guarantee period or annuity protection and the amount paid out in pension before death is less than the guaranteed pay-out. Tax at 35 per cent will be deducted.

The balance of your pension fund can be paid as a lump sum after deduction of tax at 35 per cent. If you had been drawing a low or no pension and your health was poor, inheritance tax at 40 per cent might also be charged.

Have you opted for income withdrawal?

NO ↓

No lump sum is payable from your pension scheme.

YES → The balance of your pension fund must be paid as pension to your dependant(s). If you have no dependants it can be:

• Paid tax-free to a charity you have nominated
• Transferred to the pension fund of other member(s) of the same scheme.

If you had been drawing a low or no pension, inheritance tax at 40 per cent is likely to be charged on the value of any pension or transfer.

165

❝ On death before your pension starts, a money purchase scheme typically pays out a lump sum equal to the value of the pension fund that has built up. **❞**

income withdrawal, the remaining pension fund can be paid as a lump sum if it is not being used to provide a dependant's pensions. In all these cases, tax at 35 per cent will be deducted from the pay-out.

The lump sums are payable to anyone – the recipient(s) do not have to be your dependant(s) and marital status is not an issue. The pension scheme generally asks you to nominate who you want to receive the lump sum. It does not have to follow your wishes but generally will do so. Any life insurance should be written in trust to avoid the pay-out becoming part of your estate when you die and so possibly subject to inheritance tax. But see the box on page 163 for situations where HM Revenue & Customs might seek to charge inheritance tax anyway.

Pensions and divorce

Pension rights are a valuable asset, and one which will be taken into consideration in any divorce settlement. There are various orders the court can make in the event of divorce, and similar arrangements you can adopt voluntarily.

Divorce is stressful financially as well as emotionally. Assets and income which have supported one household have to be split to support two. You might think the family home is your biggest possession, but do not overlook pensions. Pension rights can be the family's largest single asset. On the basis the government uses to compare pensions against your lifetime allowance, an occupational pension of, say £20,000 a year would be worth a capital sum of 20 x £20,000 = £400,000.

As discussed in Chapter 1, women often end up with lower pensions than men. Today, it is still more likely that a woman rather than a man will take on the care of children and elderly relatives resulting in breaks from work, and a greater likelihood of taking on part-time and low-paid jobs. As a result, a husband typically has much greater pension rights than his wife. On divorce, the wife then stands to lose:

- The opportunity to share her husband's pension in retirement or the living standard that his pension would allow.

- A widow's pension if her husband dies before her.
- A lump sum payment if her husband dies before her.

The same applies to a husband if his wife has the lion's share of the pensions. But, as that is less typical, this section is written as if the wife is the main loser. This section also applies to civil partners who break up, since the process of dissolving a civil partnership is directly equivalent to a divorce.

On divorce, the pension rights of each person may be counted alongside the other family assets to be shared out appropriately.

Unmarried and unregistered couples

If an unmarried or unregistered couple breaks up, there is no formal process of sharing out the family assets. You should try to take account of pensions, but an ex-partner with the larger pension rights may be unwilling to do this. Therefore, it is especially important that anyone in an unmarried or unregistered partnership has their own pension scheme and builds up pension rights in their own name rather than relying on their partner.

167

How pensions are taken into account

Courts must take pension rights into account when determining how a family's assets should be shared on divorce. In England, Wales and Northern Ireland, all pension rights whether built up before or during the marriage are considered. In Scotland, only rights built up during the marriage are included.

There are three ways in which the pension rights can be treated:

- **Offsetting.** The person with less in pensions may be granted a bigger share of other assets to compensate for the lost pension rights. For example, the wife might be given a large lump sum or the family home and the husband retains his pension rights in full. The main drawback with this approach is that there might not be sufficient other assets to provide the compensation.

Planning point

Pension sharing is an arrangement which both provides a clean break and ensures each of you will have some pension in retirement.

However, offsetting is likely to be the only option if the pension scheme involved is not UK-based.

- **Earmarking** (more formally called 'attachment orders'). The court can order that part of the husband's pension once it starts to be paid is handed over to the ex-wife. This could be a pension which has already started or a deferred order relating to a pension that will become payable in future. In addition or instead, the court could order that part or all of the tax-free lump sum payable at the start of retirement and/or any lump sum paid on death in service be handed over to the ex-wife. In Scotland, only lump sums not pensions can be earmarked in this way. There are several problems with this approach – for example, the ex-wife's share of any pension would stop if the husband died, or the husband might delay retiring in order to put off handing over part of the pension and/or the tax-free lump sum. Earmarking tends to be most useful as a way of providing the ex-wife with a lump sum on the death of the husband – for example, to replace maintenance payments that would then cease.
- **Pension sharing.** The court can order that part of the husband's pension rights be transferred to the

For advice on the legal aspects of divorce and separation contact Resolution (formerly Solicitors' Family Law Association). Their website is at www.resolution.org.uk or telephone 01689 820272 for further details.

ex-wife. These rights then become the wife's own and are unaffected by anything that subsequently happens in the husband's life. Pension sharing orders first became possible for divorces started on or after 1 December 2000 and their use has been steadily increasing.

Only one of these approaches can be taken in the case of any one pension scheme. But, if the husband has more than one scheme, a different approach

" On divorce, the pension rights of each person may be counted alongside the other family assets to be shared out appropriately. "

could be taken with each – for example, the death-in-service lump sum from one scheme could be earmarked for the wife to tide her over if need be until a pension secured through a pension sharing order starts.

Pensions and your family

Options for pensions on divorce

For convenience, the table is written assuming the husband has the bulk of the pension rights but applies equally if the wife or a civil partner has the main pension assets.

	Offsetting	Earmarking	Pension-sharing
Does arrangement achieve a clean break?	Yes	No	Yes
Is ex-wife unaffected by subsequent pension decisions of husband?	Yes	No	Yes
Can arrangement be used even if the family has few other non-pension assets?	No	Yes	Yes
Does it ensure the ex-wife will get a retirement pension?	No*	Maybe**	Yes
Does it ensure the ex-husband still has a retirement pension?	Yes, full pension rights retained	Yes, part of pension retained	Yes, part of pension rights retained

* If she receives a lump sum, she may be able to pay part or all into a pension scheme. But if she receives illiquid assets (such as the family home) this is unlikely to be an option
** But if husband dies, the pension stops or never becomes payable

How pension sharing works

In essence, pension sharing is very simple. One person's pension rights are reduced – the reduction is called a 'pension debit'. The other person is given a corresponding 'pension credit' with which to secure their own pension. Most pension rights can be shared, including those from occupational schemes, personal pensions (including stakeholder schemes), retirement annuity contracts and the state additional pension scheme. The main pension rights which can't be shared are the state basic pension (but see page 172) and any schemes which are not based in the UK.

Early in the divorce, each of you will be required to list for the court all your financial interests. This includes any pension schemes you belong to. You will have to contact each pension scheme and ask them to give a valuation. This will be essentially the same as the transfer value you would be given if you wanted to transfer your pension to another scheme (see Chapter 7).

This section assumes that the husband has most or all of the pension rights and the court decides that part should be transferred to the wife. Taking into account the circumstances of the couple, the length of their marriage, ages, earnings potential, other assets available, and so on, the court determines a fair share of the pension to be transferred and this is expressed as a percentage of the transfer value.

The husband has lost some of his pension rights and so stands to get a lower pension at retirement. Only the reduced rights count towards the lifetime allowance and annual allowance, so provided the husband

❝ Taking into account the length of their marriage, ages, earnings potential and other assets available the court determines a fair share of the pension to be transferred. ❞

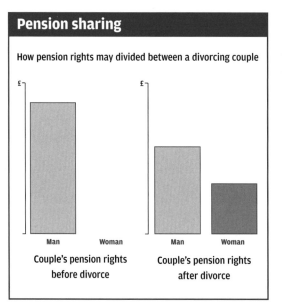

Pension sharing

How pension rights may divided between a divorcing couple

Man | Woman
Couple's pension rights before divorce

Man | Woman
Couple's pension rights after divorce

Case Study | Mel & Chris

Mel and Chris divorce. The court awards Mel a 30 per cent share of Chris' pension rights in his occupational scheme. Chris belongs to a final salary scheme and, based on his pay and years' of membership so far, has built up a pension of £12,500 a year. The scheme works out the transfer value of this pension as £77,000. Taking 30 per cent of this gives a pension debit for Chris and pension credit for Mel of £23,000. Chris' pension to date is reduced to £8,750 a year. Mel can either keep her pension credit in the scheme Chris belongs to and is told that this is expected to produce a pension of £3,200 a year at the normal pension age for the scheme. Alternatively she looks at transferring the credit to a personal pension and receives an illustration showing that it might produce a pension of £2,235 a year by her chosen pension age. Mel decides to retain the credit in Chris' scheme.

Pension credits do not count towards the annual allowance or the yearly limit on contributions that qualify for tax relief. The ex-wife can generally do one of two things with the pension credit:

- **Internal transfer.** She can become a member in her own right of her ex-husband's pension scheme. Assuming her husband had not started to draw a pension, she is treated in the same way as an early leaver who has left their rights in the old scheme (see Chapter 7) and will start to get a pension once she reaches the normal pension age for the scheme. If her husband had already started his pension, she gets a pension straight away.
- **External transfer.** If her husband had not yet started his pension, she can transfer the credit to another

can afford to, there is plenty of scope to rebuild the lost pension rights by making extra contributions.

The ex-wife has received pension rights. This increase – the pension credit – counts towards her lifetime allowance but this will only be an issue for a minority of people with very substantial pension savings.

Planning point

If your ex-spouse belongs to an unfunded public sector scheme (such as the schemes for teachers or NHS workers), a pension sharing order would give you a pension credit with that scheme. You cannot transfer the credit to another scheme but that's no hardship because public sector schemes are very secure (see Chapter 10) and offer good benefits including index-linked pensions.

For more details on how pension transfer values (from one scheme to another) are calculated, see Chapter 7, pages 144-6. The valuation for pension sharing is very similar (see this section).

scheme of her choosing. This could, for example, be her own employer's scheme if applicable or a personal pension. If the pension has already started, an external transfer is unlikely to be allowed. External transfer is also not possible from a public sector scheme which is unfunded (see page 80).

Getting advice

You can agree a financial settlement on divorce without the involvement of the courts. In that case, do make sure you still take account of the value of any pension rights. This is complicated and you are strongly advised to get help from a solicitor who will know what steps to take to obtain the necessary pension valuations and be able to call in other experts if necessary. To find a solicitor, get in touch with Resolution (formerly the Solicitors' Family Law Association) at www.resolution.org.uk.

The state basic pension and divorce

The state scheme has special rules to help people who get divorced. Broadly, you can substitute your ex-spouse's or ex-civil partner's National Insurance record for part or all of your own if this would result in a higher basic pension than you can get based on your own record. You lose this right if you subsequently remarry or enter a new civil partnership. For more information, get leaflet NP46 A guide to state pensions from The Pension Service (www.thepensionservice.gov.uk).

Your investment options

With many types of pension scheme you need to think carefully about where you want to invest your savings. The basic trade-off is between risk and return – with the aim being to strike a comfortable balance. This chapter reviews the main assets you might consider and assesses their suitability.

Investing your pension

With personal pensions, stakeholder schemes, free-standing AVC schemes, some occupational and most other money purchase schemes, it's up to you to decide how you want to invest your pension fund. The investment decisions you make will have a big impact on how much pension you eventually get.

If you belong to an occupational salary-related scheme, you are not involved in deciding how the pension fund is invested. That is also sometimes the case if you belong to a money purchase occupational scheme or save through an in-house additional voluntary contribution scheme. But with most money purchase schemes, you need to decide how to invest your savings.

THE CHOICE OF INVESTMENTS

The sort of things you can invest in depends on the type of pension scheme concerned – see table on the right.

Under the new tax rules from 6 April 2006, a single investment regime was to apply to all pension schemes. Originally it gave very wide freedom to invest in virtually any assets. This caused some excitement among people who saw the chance to invest tax-efficiently in holiday homes and second homes through their pension scheme. But at the eleventh hour, the government changed the rules.

Now, any 'self-directed pension scheme' – in other words, one where the member controls the choice of specific investments – is prohibited from investing either directly or indirectly in residential property (but see box on

Jargon buster

Self-directed pension scheme A scheme where you choose the specific investments the fund invests in. The main examples are self-invested personal pensions (SIPPs) and small self-administered schemes (SSASs).

Prohibited assets Residential property and possessions such as cars, fine wines, art and antiques. Self-directed pension schemes are taxed prohibitively if they invest in these assets.

Investment fund A wide range of different shares and/or other investments chosen by a fund manager. The investments are purchased by pooling your money with that of lots of other investors.

page 176) or possessions such as cars, fine wine, art and antiques. If your scheme were to invest in such assets, you personally would be charged 40 per cent tax on the value of the assets, the scheme would face severe penalties. For more about self-directed pension schemes, see page 187 onwards.

Although in theory other types of pension scheme that are not 'self-directed' can still invest widely, in practice they are bound by other rules to invest prudently and are generally unlikely to use prohibited assets. With most of these schemes, your choice is limited to selecting investment funds.

How you can invest your pension fund

Type of scheme	Your investment choice
Occupational money purchase scheme	With many schemes, investments are chosen by the people running the scheme and you have no choice. With some, you can choose from a (usually limited) range of investment funds
In-house AVC scheme	With some schemes there is no choice and your contributions are automatically paid into an account or fund selected by the people running the scheme. With others, you can choose from a (usually limited) range of investment funds
Free-standing AVC scheme	You choose from a range of investment funds offered by the insurance company offering the scheme
Personal pensions (other than SIPPs) and retirement annuity contracts	You choose from a range of investment funds offered by the insurance company offering the scheme
Stakeholder schemes	You normally choose from a limited range of investment funds offered by the insurance company. If you make no choice, your contributions are automatically invested in a 'lifestyle fund' – see page 183
SIPPs and SSAS	You choose the specific investments which may be, for example, investment funds (which can be unit trusts and investment trusts, not just funds offered by insurance companies), shares, commercial property and so on. You may not invest in residential property or possessions such as cars, fine wine, art and antiques.

INVESTMENTS – THE BIG PICTURE

The return on your investments will be the single biggest factor determining the size of your pension fund at retirement and the amount of pension you can buy. But unfortunately you can't know in advance what that return will be and there is no fool-proof way of picking tomorrow's investment winners.

Many people spend a lot of time trying to spot the investment funds they think will perform best but academic research shows that there is only a very weak correlation between current and future fund performance. Moreover, academics reckon that the major influence on your return is not the individual funds you pick but the balance between broad type of investments, called 'asset classes':

- **Cash** This refers to deposits similar to the accounts you would have with a bank or building society. Your money earns interest and, generally, you cannot lose any of your original investment (your 'capital').
- **Bonds** These are loans to governments or companies. The borrower agrees to pay your money back at a set future date and in the meantime you may earn interest. You do not have to hold the bonds until repayment – instead you can sell them on the stock market. The price you can sell at depends on market conditions and could be more or less than the amount you invested. There is also some risk that the borrower might fail to pay

Real estate investment trusts

Although a SIPP or SSAS may not generally invest in residential property, the government has said that they – like other types of pension scheme – will be able to invest in real estate investment trusts (REITs) once they become available from January 2007. These are a new type of investment fund that invests in a broad spread of different properties which may be residential, commercial or both.

Jargon buster

Capital The amount of money you originally invest.

Bond A loan to either a government or a company which can be bought and sold on a stock market.

Gilts The name for bonds issued by the UK government.

Equities Another name for shares in companies.

Shares An investment that makes you a part-owner of a company along with all the other shareowners. The return you get depends on how well the company performs.

Capital risk The likelihood of losing part or all of your original investment and/or gains you have already built up

the interest or repay the capital as agreed. This risk is very low in the case of loans to the UK government (called 'gilts').

- **Property** This means investing in things like office blocks and shopping centres either directly or by owning shares in companies that hold and run such properties. Your return is generated by the rents that tenants pay and any increase in the value of the properties. But, if property prices fall or expenses exceed the rental income, you could make a loss.
- **Equities** This means shares in companies. When you buy shares, you become part-owner of the company along with all the other shareholders. The return you get depends on how well the company performs. You may receive dividends (a slice of the company's profits paid out as income to shareholders) and/or a gain if the shares' price rises over the time you have held them. If the share price falls, you make a loss.

The asset classes above are listed in order of increasing 'capital risk' – in other words, the likelihood of losing your capital or previous growth. The assets are also listed in increasing order of the return you are likely to get. This is no coincidence. A fundamental rule of investing is that risk and return go hand in hand. The higher the likely return, the greater the risk. The lower the risk,

The trade off between risk and return

Risk escalates with each asset class plotted on the chart below, although the return on your investment grows too.

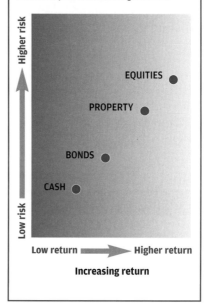

the lower the return. It's easy to see why this is so. Ideally everyone would like to invest with no risk at all. If investors are to be tempted away from very safe investments there must be a reward for doing so. That reward is the prospect of a higher return.

The chart above illustrates where the asset classes typically lie in relation to each other if you were to plot their returns against the risk involved.

Balancing risk and return

Most people do not like taking risks. So it could be tempting to save for retirement by putting all your money into cash assets. But reducing capital risk in this way increases the amount you need to save and could make it impossible for you to afford your pension target.

The chart below shows how much a man aged 30 might need to start saving each month to produce a pension of £10,000 a year in today's money by age 65 given different returns on his investment. If he chose investments paying on average 3 per cent a year, he would need to start saving £431 a month (over £5,000 a year). This is almost double the amount he would need to save if he opted for investments producing an average return of 7 per cent a year. But the higher-returning assets will almost certainly involve more capital risk than the lower-returning assets.

Managing the amount of risk

Saving for retirement is a long-term goal. The table on page 185 shows that, over most long-term periods, equities have tended to produce significantly higher returns than gilts or cash. However, this has not been true for all periods. A sharp drop in share prices between 2000 and 2002 shows up in the return over 10 years when gilts unusually out-performed equities. There are several important points to note:

- **The past is no guide to the future.** Although past trends can help you to form a view about what might happen in future, they are not a

Saving rates

The chart shows how much a man might need to save each month from age 30 to produce £10,000 a year pension by age 65 with differing rates of return.

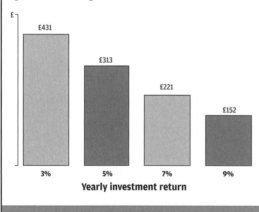

£431 — 3%
£313 — 5%
£221 — 7%
£152 — 9%

Yearly investment return

Assumes: charges average 1 per cent a year, price inflation averages 2.5 per cent a year, earnings inflation averages 4 per cent a year, monthly savings increase once a year in line with earnings inflation and pension increases in line with price inflation once it starts to be paid.

reliable guide. The future could turn out to be different.

- **Risks can and do materialise.** Although there is a consistent trend of equities outperforming gilts and cash over most long-term periods, this does not mean that equities were the best performer in every year. In recent times, there have been major share price collapses in 1974, 1987 and 2000.
- **Different assets behave differently.** For example, looking at the return over 10 years in the table on page 185, not only was the return on equities lower at 5 per cent than the average for most other periods, but the return on gilts was unusually high.
- **Spread your money.** It makes sense to spread your money across assets which are likely to respond differently to economic events so that if one type slumps, others may be doing well. And, because risks do materialise from time to time, you either want to be in a position to sit tight and ride out a bad patch or, if you are close to retiring, to avoid the more risky investments.

How to manage investment risk

- **Don't be recklessly cautious.** If you avoid all capital risk, you increase the risk of being unable to meet your investment targets. You also increase the risk that your investments might not grow enough even to beat inflation.
- **Don't put all your eggs in one basket.** Have a spread of different types of investment – some equities, some property, some bonds and some cash. You can achieve this by, say, choosing a mix of different investment funds or a single fund that automatically holds a mix of different assets – see page 180 onwards.
- **Match the risks to your circumstances and temperament.** Normally you should take less risk, the lower the amount you have to invest. When you are young, you can usually afford to take more risks with your pension fund than when you are older. This is for two reasons. Firstly, you can ride out even a fairly lengthy slump in share prices because you have a long time to go until you need to convert your pension fund into income. Secondly, if you do make losses, you still have many earning years left which gives you a chance to replace your losses. As you get older, you should generally reduce your exposure to risk. Whatever your age, you need to be comfortable with the degree of risk you take – there is no point being fully invested in shares if every movement of the stock market will keep you awake at night.
- **Lock in your gains as retirement approaches.** Protect yourself from a share slump just as you need to cash in your investments to buy a pension. Do this by shifting your fund away from equities and into bonds and cash over, say, the ten year run-up to starting your pension. 'Lifestyle funds' (see page 183) make this shift for you automatically.

Examples of investment funds

This table shows how the main investment funds differ in terms of risk.

Asset class	Type of fund	Description	Risk indication
Cash	Money market	Money in the fund is mainly on deposit earning interest. Normally risk of losing your capital	LOW RISK
Bonds	Gilt	Invested mainly in gilts. Value of fund can fall as well as rise because gilts being bought and sold on stock market	
	UK and fixed interest	Invested mainly in gilts other bonds. Value of fund can fall as well as rise because bonds being bought and sold on stock market	
Mix of asset classes	Protected/ Guaranteed	Fund aims to return either all or a set percentage of your capital but also give you some chance of stockmarket growth	
	Cautious managed	Maximum 60 per cent of the fund in equities (which can include overseas as well as UK shares). Rest in bonds and cash	
	With profit	Your investment earns bonuses which are linked to an underlying fund invested in equities, property, bonds and cash	
	Balanced managed	Maximum 85 per cent of the fund in equities (with at least some in overseas shares). Rest in bonds and cash	
	Lifestyle	Fund starts by being invested mainly in equities but, in the 10 years or so up to drawing your pension, automatically shifts to bonds and cash in order to lock in your past gains	
Property	Property	At the time of writing, invested mainly in commercial property. Real estate investment trusts (REITs) are due to be introduced which can invest instead or as well as in residential property	
Equities	UK all companies	Invested mainly in the shares of UK companies	
	Tracker	Invested to mimic the performance of a selected stock market index	
	Global equities	Invested mainly in shares of companies from around the world	
	Europe	Invested mainly in the shares of companies based in continental Europe. Some funds include the UK	
	UK smaller companies	Invested mainly in the shares of small UK companies	
	Global emerging markets	Invested mainly in shares of companies in countries whose economies are developing or growing fast	
	Asia Pacific	Invested in the shares of companies based in Asian countries around the Pacific. Some funds exclude Japan which increases risk	HIGH RISK

INVESTMENT FUNDS

Investing in different asset classes helps you spread risk. Equally, within each asset class, it is important to have a spread of different shares, bonds, and so on. Then, if one investment fails, it has only a small impact on your overall fund. Building up your own spread of investments is costly and requires knowledge and confidence. For most people, investment funds are the most cost-effective and convenient way to hold a spread of investments. These are ready-made portfolios that automatically give you a wide spread of investments. You invest by buying units in a fund and the return you get is in proportion to the number of units you hold. The table on the left gives an overview of the main funds available. For more details, see pages 181 to 185.

Money market funds

The money in the fund is put on deposit to earn interest. Because the fund is large, it can normally get much better rates than you would at your bank or building society. Money market funds are particularly useful in the run up to retirement when you want to avoid any risk of losing your capital or previous gains.

Gilt and fixed interest funds

The investments in these funds are gilts, corporate bonds (in other words, bonds issued by companies) and similar investments, all of which are known collectively as 'fixed interest'.

A single bond typically offers a fixed income and usually a set capital gain (or loss) payable at the set date when the bond is repaid. A fund investing in bonds does not offer the same guaranteed returns, because the fund manager will be constantly buying and selling different bonds. However, because of the nature of the bonds, the fund as a whole provides a reasonably stable return. Over the long-term, this is unlikely to be as exciting as the return on shares, so you generally do not want too much of your money in bonds if you are a long way from retirement. But as retirement approaches it may be sensible gradually to switch your investments away from volatile equities to more stable bonds in order to lock in past growth.

Protected/guaranteed funds

These funds are examples of a group of investments more widely referred to as 'structured products'. They use a combination of two (or sometimes more) types of financial product to produce an investment that can deliver a particular aim. With protected and guaranteed funds, the aim is to guarantee the return of part or all of your capital but also give you the chance to benefit from stock market growth.

These funds can be structured in different ways. Here is one example of

> **" You will normally have to invest at least some of your money in share-based investments that offer the chance of higher returns. "**

a guaranteed fund. Say, you invest £1,000. £950 might be invested in a bond or put on deposit to provide a fixed return of £1,000 at a set future date. This provides the return of your capital. The remaining £50 is used to buy investments linked to a stock market index that will make a gain if the stock market rises by the set future date but return nothing if the stock market falls. Once the set date is reached, the cycle starts again.

With a protected fund, only part of your capital is protected. For example, some of your money buys a bond that will provide a fixed return equal to 90 per cent of your capital. This leaves a larger sum to be invested in stock market linked products and so increases the gains if the stock market rises. But, if the stock market fails to rise, you lose some of your capital.

With-profits schemes and funds

Traditional with-profits pension schemes were an alternative to the sort where you bought units in an investment scheme and there are still some with-profits schemes like this. They are offered by insurance companies and some friendly societies.

Your money is invested by the scheme provider in its with-profits fund which holds a diverse range of shares, bonds, property, and so on. Your return depends largely on how well the fund grows, but also on other factors such as the expenses incurred by the provider, whether it has to pay out some of the profits to its shareholders, and so on. The provider also uses a process of 'smoothing' to avoid sharp fluctuations in your return from one year to the next. Smoothing means holding back some of the return from good years to top up the pay-out in bad years. The scheme's actuary decides how much is available to be paid to the scheme members each year.

Your return is in the form of two types of bonus. Reversionary bonuses are added to your scheme regularly, usually once a year. A terminal bonus is added at the time you convert your investment into pension. The level of future bonuses is not guaranteed and can be varied from year to year or even missed altogether. Once a reversionary bonus has been added to your plan, in general it can't be taken

 For more information on asset performance see publications such as Money Management and Money Observer, available from larger newsagents.

away, so your plan should be on a constantly growing path. However, if you transfer your pension fund out of the scheme before your planned pension date, charges are likely to be deducted from the transfer value and may recoup some of the bonuses you had previously received.

These days, many with-profits schemes are organised, like most other investment funds, on a unit-linked basis. The with-profits fund is just one of the many different investment funds you can choose from and your money buys units in the fund. The value of the units increases in line with the bonuses as they are declared. But, instead of the provider's expenses being implicit in the level of bonuses, they are separated out and charged separately in the usual way

Planning point

If you like the idea of stock market growth but low or no capital risk, a protected or guaranteed fund could be the answer. However, these funds are varied and complex - make sure you understand how the fund works and the nature of the guarantee or protection before you invest. Be aware too that any gains you make will be less than if you had invested directly in equities because guaranteed and protected funds have extra charges and the return is linked only to stock market growth without the benefit of any dividend income.

that applies with any unit-linked fund (see page 186). This makes unit-linked with-profits funds more transparent than the traditional with-profits schemes.

Lifestyle funds

These are a relatively new concept. When you start your pension scheme, your money is invested in a fund which takes into account your attitude towards risk and the length of time until your pension is planned to start. A mix of shares, bonds, property and cash is chosen to reflect these factors and then automatically adjusted as time goes by. For example, if you take out a scheme in your 30s and plan to retire at age 65 and are comfortable with a reasonably high level of risk, your fund might be invested initially entirely in shares. When you are around age 50, the fund manager may start to switch some of your investments into bonds. By the time you are 60, say a quarter of your fund might be in bonds. During the last five years, the manager may start shifting you into cash as well, so that by 65 your fund might be invested, say 25 per cent in cash and 75 per cent in bonds, with no shares at all.

The advantage of a lifestyle fund is that you avoid any worry about making investment decisions but will automatically have been exposed to stock market growth while you were younger and have had your gains locked in as retirement approached.

183

Property funds

Property funds often invest in the shares of property companies rather than holding property direct. In general, property is considered to be a lower-risk, more steady investment than equities. But property, if held direct, is fairly illiquid because it takes time to find a buyer and organise a sale. Therefore, the terms and conditions of the fund may allow for a delay if necessary of up to six or 12 months before your money can be released.

Equity funds

These are funds investing mainly or wholly in company shares. There is a huge range to choose from, for example:

- **UK shares.** This lets you participate in the performance of companies whose prospects are likely to depend largely on the performance of the UK economy.
- **Overseas shares.** Here you are hooking into the performance of economies overseas. There is an extra layer of risk because the return will initially be in a foreign currency and has to be converted into sterling. Therefore, movements in the exchange rate affect the return you get.
- **Small company shares.** These funds offer the chance of high returns because small companies may have the potential to grow very fast but equally there is extra risk because small companies often find it harder to compete and may fail.
- **Specialist funds.** These may invest in, say, companies that trade commodities or energy. Some funds seek out companies that are in poor shape now but look as if they have a good chance of recovery. Specialist funds are often high risk.
- **Ethical funds.** Some funds either seek out companies that have good trade, employment or environmental practices or avoid companies that participate in, say, the arms trade, tobacco, alcohol or gambling. Check the ethical aims of individual funds to find the ones that match your own ethical stance or religious beliefs. For information, consult the Ethical Investment Research Information Service (EIRIS) at www.eiris.org.

Planning point

Some financial advisers suggest that the percentage of your pension fund invested in equities should be roughly 100 less your age. For example, if you are 30, you should have 100-30 = 70 per cent of your fund in share-based investments. (But not all advisers agree with this rule of thumb.)

Tracker funds

With most investment funds, the fund manager tries to select the underlying shares or other investments that he or she believes will give the best returns. This involves continuously monitoring the relevant markets and being prepared to switch investments as conditions change. This is called 'active' fund management. Of course, there is no guarantee that the fund manager will succeed in outguessing the markets – indeed there is some evidence that active fund management does not beat the market at all. And the downside of active fund management is the costs involved in paying for so much input from the fund manager and the charges for frequent sales and purchases of the investments (see page 186). As a result, some funds have opted for 'passive' management.

Passive managers run tracker funds. With a tracker fund, the main input from the manager is when the fund is first set up. The underlying investments are selected to mimic a particular stock market index – for example, the FTSE 100 Index. This could mean the fund invests in all the shares that make up that index or invests in a selection of investments that give a close approximation. The fund is then left to track the index, with no attempt made to identify and switch to the expected best performers. Because there is less

manager involvement and less buying and selling of investments, tracker fund charges should be lower than charges levied by actively managed funds.

CHARGES

Chapter 5 showed how charges can have a big impact on your eventual pension fund (see page 107). Charges come in a wide variety of forms – see page 186.

> ### Jargon buster
>
> **Active fund management** Trying to improve the returns from an investment fund by constantly monitoring and trading the underlying investments in an attempt to pick the best performers.
> **Passive fund management** Setting up an investment fund to mimic the performance of a stock market index.
> **FTSE 100 Index** A measure of stock market performance based on the share prices of the 100 largest companies quoted on the London Stock Exchange.

Long-term returns from different assets

	Yearly investment return over and above inflation over the period to end 2004				
	1 year	10 years	20 years	50 years	105 years
Equities	8.8%	5.0%	7.2%	6.3%	5.1%
Gilts	3.6%	6.5%	6.1%	1.7%	1.1%
Cash	1.1%	3.0%	4.2%	1.9%	1.0%

Typical pension scheme charges

Type of charge	Description
Investment fund charges	
Bid-offer spread	The difference between the higher 'offer price' at which you buy units and the lower 'bid price' at which you sell them. Typically the spread is around 5 to 6 per cent. 'Single priced' funds do not have this charge – they buy and sell units at the same price and levy charges in other ways.
Exit charge	A charge when you sell your units, often levied only if you sell during the first few years. Most commonly used by single-priced funds.
Annual management charge	A yearly charge deducted from the fund to cover the cost of managing the investments. Typically around 1 to 1.5 per cent a year of the value of the fund. Expect to pay less than 1 per cent for a tracker fund.
Fund expenses	The dealing costs of buying and selling investments in the fund and charges for their safekeeping are deducted direct from the fund and not normally counted with the other charges.
Other charges commonly levied by insurance companies	
Policy fee or administration charge	A one-off or regular charge to cover the costs of setting up and/or running the scheme.
Unit allocation	A given percentage of each payment is used to buy units. The percentage may be lower in the earlier years of the plan and/or if you pay, say, monthly rather than yearly. Don't be misled by an allocation of over 100 per cent – it generally means 100 per cent of your contributions after deducting a policy fee or other charges.
Capital units	Be wary of schemes that offer special units during the first year or two of the scheme – they usually have a much higher annual management charge (say 3 to 5 per cent a year) and this higher charge normally applies throughout the life of the scheme.
Surrender or transfer charges	You may be credited with only part of the value of your pension fund if you stop paying in regular contributions or transfer the scheme during the early years.
Market value adjustment (MVA)	If you transfer a with-profits scheme, your fund's transfer value may be reduced if the investment conditions are poor at the time of the transfer. The aim of the market value adjustment (MVA) is to claw back part of the bonuses already credited to your scheme to ensure a fair distribution of the with-profits fund between people who are transferring out and those who are left invested in the fund.

SELF-DIRECTED PENSION SCHEMES

Despite the government u-turn on pension schemes investing in residential property, cars, antiques and so on ('prohibited assets'), the tax rules still allow for a wide choice of investments. But to benefit from the widest choice you will need to take out either a:

- **Self invested personal pension (SIPP).** This is a type of personal pension suitable for individuals who want a high degree of control over their pension scheme, or
- **Small self-administered scheme (SSAS).** This is a type of occupational scheme particularly useful if you run your own small company and want to use the pension scheme to help your business. Your company is the 'sponsoring employer' of the scheme which opens up various options not available with personal pensions.

The SIPP or SSAS itself is an empty pension wrapper. The firm offering it is selling you the framework and administration for your scheme. You then fill it up with the investments of your choice.

Both SIPPs and SSASs usually involve substantial charges for setting

> **" SIPPs and SSASs are allowed to invest in any investments apart from prohibited assets. "**

up and running the schemes. Typically, you'll pay a set-up fee and annual management charge for the SIPP or SSAS framework and then transaction charges each time you buy and sell investments plus a variety of other incidental costs. Charges generally make these schemes uneconomic unless you have a minimum of around £100,000 to invest. However, low-cost SIPPs are increasingly coming onto the market – often set up and operated over the Internet. They give you a wide choice of investment funds, but not other investments (such as commercial property). Charges are much lower, making these types of SIPP suitable for investments from, say, £25,000 upwards.

Jargon buster

Sponsoring employer The employer who sets up and contributes to an occupational scheme.

For more information on pension scheme rules and regulations contact HM Revenue & Customs, website www.hmrc.gov.uk/pensionschemes.

Investments

SIPPs and SSASs are allowed to invest in any investments apart from prohibited assets. This can include, for example, direct investment in any types of shares (quoted on a stock exchange, unquoted, UK or overseas), gilts, bonds, commercial land and buildings, and so on. But, if a SSAS buys shares in the sponsoring employer's company, the value of the shares must be less than 5 per cent of the value of the pension scheme's assets. You can also invest some or all of the scheme in investment funds choosing from the very wide range offered by unit trust and investment trust managers, as well as insurance companies.

> " The overriding aim of the scheme is to provide you with a pension for life. "

The scheme might hold assets which you, your family or household use, in which case a value is put on the benefit you get and you personally are charged tax on that benefit. For example, a scheme might hold commercial premises which you decide to use for personal storage while they are standing vacant. You would be deemed to be getting a benefit in kind equal to the commercial rent you would otherwise be paying and have to pay tax at 40 per cent on that amount. You could

Planning point

Even if you stick to investment funds, a SIPP gives you a much wider choice of funds than an ordinary personal pension.

reduce the tax bill by paying rent to the pension scheme.

There is no taxable benefit if the scheme receives a full commercial rent for the use of its assets. For example, the scheme could buy your business premises and rent them back to you on commercial terms. Your business could claim tax relief on the rent paid, the rent would be tax-free in the hands of the pension scheme and the scheme would pay no capital gains tax on the property when it was eventually sold.

The overriding aim of the scheme is to provide you with a pension for life and the investments must be compatible with that aim. Therefore, the scheme must have enough liquid assets to pay your pension when it falls due. This could mean, for example, selling property before that day arrives.

If the assets in the scheme are not compatible with providing the pensions due, HM Revenue & Customs could challenge the arrangement, clawing back previous tax reliefs and imposing penalty tax charges.

Buying from and selling to you

There are no restrictions on the scheme buying its investments from you or anyone connected with you or selling investments to you or your associates. But the purchase or sale must be on the same commercial terms that would apply if an unconnected person were involved.

Borrowing by the pension scheme

The pension scheme is allowed to borrow money in order to buy assets, but all such borrowings must not come to more than half the value of the assets in the pension fund just before the loan was taken out. For example, a scheme with assets worth £100,000 could at most borrow £50,000.

Loans from the scheme

Pension schemes may not lend to their members or people connected with their members, so for example you can't borrow money from your SIPP.

But occupational schemes, like SSASs, can lend to their sponsoring employer, provided all such loans come to no more than half the value of the pension fund and various other conditions are met.

Pension scheme investments

Pension schemes may not invest in residential property or assets, such as classic cars, wine and antiques. But this does not mean you have to stick just to investment funds. Here are some of the more unusual investments which you are allowed to invest in:

- Gold bullion (but not, for example, gold jewellery.
- Hotels, except where they provide accommodation on a timeshare basis.
- Children's homes.
- Student halls of residence (but not normal flats and houses let out to students).
- Residential care homes.
- Hospitals and hospices.
- Prisons.
- Job-related residential accommodation occupied by an employee, for example, a caretaker's flat. The employee must not be a member or the pension scheme or connected to a member of the scheme.
- Residential accommodation used in connection with business premises, such as a flat over a shop occupied by the trader. Once again it must not be occupied by a member of the pension scheme or anyone connected to a scheme member.

MORE INFORMATION

Investment funds

You can find further information about the various investment funds available for pension scheme investments from:

- Pension scheme literature and providers' websites. These should describe each fund and the point out any significant risks involved.
- Independent websites, for example, TrustNet (www.trustnet.com) and Standard & Poors (www.funds-sp.com)
- Personal finance magazines, such as *Money Management* and *Pensions Management*.

❝ If you are not confident making your own choice of funds, get advice either from the agent of the provider you are investing with or an independent financial adviser. ❞

If you are not confident making your own choice of funds, get advice either from the salesperson or agent of the provider you are investing with or an independent financial adviser. For more information about using an adviser, see pages 121-2.

SIPPs and SSASs

SIPPs are offered by a range of companies, for example, insurers, fund managers, actuaries and stockbrokers. SSASs are more specialist schemes offered by some insurers and actuaries. For a list of providers and their schemes, see the regular surveys published by *Money Management* magazine or get advice from an independent financial adviser.

Using a pension scheme to support your business is a complex matter with many aspects and trade-offs to take into account. Therefore, get specialist advice from an accountant or independent financial adviser.

Is your pension safe?

Pensions have had a bad press recently. With scandals and shortfalls, closed schemes and cutbacks, it seems that they are far less reliable than they used to be. Should we really worry? What are the signs to look for? What can you do to keep your pension on track?

Protecting your pension

Pensions are hardly out of the news these days and the stories always seem bad – schemes closing, pension fund black holes, work till you drop. Coming on top of some high-profile scandals over the last two decades, it is hardly surprising that many people have lost confidence in pensions.

You may wonder whether it is worth saving for retirement at all. But it is important to keep a proper perspective. Yes, with any scheme, there is some risk of ending up with less pension than you had expected. But that is much less likely to be a problem than the virtual certainty of eking out an impoverished old age if you make no savings for retirement at all. And, because of the tax advantages and contributions from your employer, occupational pension schemes remain for most people the best way to build up those savings.

Nevertheless, it is important to understand the risks you face, the help available if they materialise and what you may be able to do to avert problems.

YOUR STATE PENSION

The government is unlikely to go bust and be unable to pay the pension it owes you. In that sense, state pensions are very secure. But retirement planning means taking decisions now that will be a long time bearing fruit. Therefore, it is important to be able to plan with certainty. It's here that the state has a habit of letting you down.

❝ What the state says today could be very different by the time you become a pensioner. ❞

The state system has been changed on numerous occasions and all too often change means cutbacks – see the table, right. In general, changes have been phased in so that people close to retirement are affected less or not at all. But if you are relatively young now, you should be aware that what the state promises today could be very different by the time you become a pensioner. Of course, if the Turner Commission proposals (see Introduction) are taken up, future state pensions might be higher though you might have to wait longer to get them.

State pension cutbacks

State pension provision has changed significantly over the past twenty years.

Date	Change	Effect
1980	Link to earnings inflation cut	Pensions being paid had been increased each year in line with the higher of earnings or price inflation. Now they are increased only in line with prices. Pensioners are becoming progressively poorer relative to people in work.
1988	State earnings related pension scheme (SERPS) pensions cut	Lower state additional pension for people retiring and their widows (and subsequently widowers and bereaved civil partners).
1988	Introduction of contracting out on a money purchase basis	Contracting out this new way might leave you better or worse off.
1997	Changes to contracting out through a salary-related scheme	Before the change, you could not lose by contracting out this way. After the change, you could be either better or worse off.
1997	Reduced protection against inflation for contracted-out pensions	Contracted-out pensions being paid no longer fully protected against inflation – only inflation up to a maximum of 5 per cent a year.
2002	SERPS replaced by the state second pension	No-one worse off and carers, some low earners and some people with long-term illness or disabilities better off. However, the government originally intended S2P would become a flat-rate scheme and if this does eventually happen moderate to high earners would be likely to lose out.
2005	Reduced protection against inflation for contracted-out pensions	Contracted-out salary-related only have to be protected against inflation up to a maximum of 2.5 per cent a year. Contracted-out money purchase pensions no longer have to be protected against inflation at all.
2010 to 2020	Women's state pension age being raised from 60 to 65	Women have to wait longer to receive their state pension.

OCCUPATIONAL PENSION SCHEMES

There are two main risks with occupational schemes: first that the employer or someone else might embezzle money that was intended to pay for pensions; and secondly that, without any dishonesty, the scheme cannot pay the pension it has promised. The first risk can affect any sort of scheme but the second is peculiar to salary-related schemes.

Keeping pensions safe

Occupational pension schemes must normally either be statutory schemes or set up under trust. A statutory scheme is set up under an Act of Parliament and is the normal arrangement for most public sector schemes – covering, for example, NHS workers, teachers, the police, and so on. Usually these schemes are unfunded and the pensions derive their security from the fact that future taxpayers can be called upon to pay for them – but see also the section entitled Renegotiating the pension promise on page 198.

A private sector scheme is nearly always set up as a trust, a device which ensures the scheme is at arm's length from the employer and his or her business. With any trust, there are three key players:

- **The sponsor who sets up the trust** – in this case the employer. The employer usually decides on the initial benefits and rules of the scheme (which may later be altered if the rules allow for this).
- **The beneficiaries** who are the scheme members. These are the people for whom the trust has been set up. The aim of the trust is to provide them with pensions and other benefits. The beneficiaries include not just the 'active' members who are working for the employer now, but also people with preserved pensions and people who might benefit if, say, a scheme member dies. The employer is usually also a beneficiary who can, in certain

---

Planning point

You can get actively involved in ensuring your pension scheme is run well by standing for election as a trustee. Most occupational schemes must have at least some trustees nominated by the scheme members. To find out more, talk to the pension scheme administrator at work.

 For details of how personal pension schemes are regulated, see page 200. See also Chapter 9 for advice on managing investment risk.

circumstances, receive money back from the scheme.

- **The trustees** who have the task of looking after the trust property – in this case, the pension fund – and making sure that it is used in accordance with the scheme rules for the good of the beneficiaries.

The trustees are responsible for the running of the scheme but can employ help and have a duty to seek specialist help as required. They normally appoint a scheme administrator to handle day-to-day matters, investment managers to advise on investment strategy and the selection of investments, an actuary to evaluate the assets and liabilities and advise on the level of contributions required, a lawyer to advise on legal aspects and an auditor to check the accounts.

The trustees and the advisers are all responsible for seeing that the employer meets its obligations to the scheme, the scheme is properly run and blowing the whistle if they suspect there is something wrong. They are supported and overseen by the Pensions Regulator – see Box, top right.

The aim is that the trustees, advisers and Pensions Regulator will together create a tough regulatory framework that will ensure no-one can steal from or defraud the pension scheme. But, in those cases where it does happen, there is a compensation scheme.

The Pensions Regulator

If you suspect your pension scheme is breaking the law or your employer is not acting properly in relation to the scheme (for example, failing to pay in contributions on time), tell the Pensions Regulator – see www.thepensionsregulator.gov.uk for more information.

This is the official body which regulates all work-based pension schemes (occupational schemes and also those personal pensions and stakeholder schemes organised through your workplace). It promotes good practice, monitors risks, investigates schemes if something seems to be wrong, has powers to put things right and can fine and prosecute individual wrong-doers.

❝ The aim is that the trustees, advisers and Pension Regulator will together create a tough regulatory framework. ❞

The Fraud Compensation Fund can pay out where an occupational pension scheme's assets have been reduced as the result of dishonesty. The scheme is expected first to do all it can to recover the lost assets. Where a shortfall is left, the compensation scheme can step in. The fund is financed by a levy on all occupational pension schemes.

195

Failing to meet the pension promise

In a salary-related scheme, you are promised a given amount of pension worked out according to the pension formula for your scheme (see Chapter 4). Enough has to be paid into the scheme to ensure that each member's pension can be paid as it falls due. You are usually required to pay some contributions but the employer pays the balance of the cost. The employer's contributions rise and fall in line as the cost of providing the promised pensions increases or reduces. The scheme actuary works out the level of contributions required based on assumptions about, for example, how well the invested contributions might grow and how long the pensions will have to be paid out (in other words, the life expectancy of the members). In a pension scheme where most of the members are a long way from retirement, the actuary usually assumes that the pension scheme will be invested largely in shares which, as discussed in Chapter 9, tend to be more suitable for the long-term than lower-risk but lower-returning investments.

In theory, the scheme is simultaneously required to have enough in the fund to meet all its obligations if the scheme came to an end today (in other words, if the scheme were to 'wind up'). In that case you would be entitled to a preserved pension or transfer value as described in Chapter 7. To be sure of doing this the pension fund would have to be invested in assets which offered a known and stable return (in other words, gilts).

In practice, there is a lot of leeway in the way this funding requirement is applied and schemes are allowed to hold a high proportion of shares. But, at any point in time, share prices could be in a short-term fall. Therefore, a scheme can be broadly

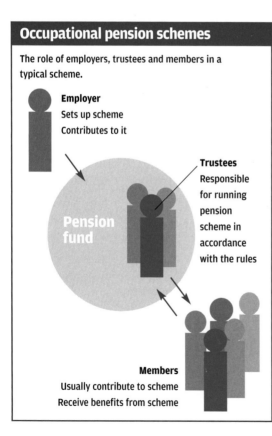

Occupational pension schemes

The role of employers, trustees and members in a typical scheme.

Employer
Sets up scheme
Contributes to it

Pension fund

Trustees
Responsible for running pension scheme in accordance with the rules

Members
Usually contribute to scheme
Receive benefits from scheme

on track to pay its long-term promises but have too little in the fund to meet all its obligations if the scheme were wound up today.

Normally, if there is a shortfall when a pension scheme is wound up, this is a debt on the employer who must pump extra money into the scheme. But this is not possible if the employer is insolvent. Between 1997 and April 2005, it is estimated that some 85,000 members of occupational salary-related schemes lost some of their promised pension because their employer went out of business leaving a big hole in the pension fund. As a result two compensation schemes were established:

- **Financial Assistance Scheme (FAS).** This scheme has been set up and funded by the government to provide help for those pension scheme members in greatest need where their pension scheme started to wind up during the period 1 January 1997 to 5 April 2005, the scheme was under-funded and their employer is insolvent. The trustees of the scheme make the application to the fund and help is directed generally at members who are within three years of their scheme's normal pension age or older.

" In a salary-related scheme, you are promised a given amount of pension. "

- **Pension Protection Fund (PPF).** This scheme takes over to provide compensation where a scheme winds up on or after 6 April 2005 with too little in the fund and an insolvent employer. In general, compensation would ensure that existing pensioners carry on getting the full amount of their pension and that other scheme members get 90 per cent of their promised pension up to a maximum limit (£28,764 at age 65 in 2006-7). The PPF is financed by a levy on occupational salary-related schemes.

Both schemes have been criticised - for example, the FAS for being too poorly funded to help adequately all members who have lost out and the PPF for providing too little compensation for those who retire before age 65.

Public sector pension schemes are not covered by the above compensation schemes because they are instead ultimately backed by tax revenues.

To find out more about the Pension Protection Fund (PPF) and the scope of its provisions, see the website www.pensionprotectionfund.org.uk.

Renegotiating the pension promise

Many final salary schemes are realising they cannot afford to provide the pensions they had promised because the cost of the pension scheme is increasing dramatically. There are various reasons for this, in particular the fact that on average employees are now expected to live much longer than originally thought. Employers are looking at ways to cut the cost, for example, closing schemes to new members, stopping existing members from building up further benefits, switching to career average or money purchase schemes and/or trying to persuade workers to retire later.

Looking at the bigger picture, it is probably inevitable that these sorts of changes will happen at some time given that we are all tending to live longer. But, at your personal level, a reduction in the pension you had been led to expect as part of the overall remuneration package for your job is effectively the same as a pay cut.

If your employer is trying to change your pension scheme, there might not be a lot a lot you can do stop it. But you should try taking the following steps:

- **Check your contract of employment.** Does it give you the right to a particular type or amount of pension? (Most contracts don't.)
- **Contact the trustees.** They may have the power to force the scheme to wind up rather than simply be altered. If the scheme is wound up, the employer must pay in extra contributions if there is a shortfall in the pension fund. Since this could be very costly, your employer might be forced to think again about changing the scheme.
- **Contact your union or staff association.** They may be able to negotiate a better deal regarding the pension scheme.
- **Talk to your employer.** Even if you can't stop the changes, you might be able to negotiate a compensating pay rise or extra pension contributions in your case.

Members of money purchase schemes

If you belong to a money purchase scheme, there is no pension promise, so you are generally not affected by employers cutting back on and changing their pension schemes. But that's because you already bear the risks that employers are now trying to offload. As life expectancy increases, annuity rates tend to fall, so you either have to pay more into your pension scheme or end up with a lower pension when you retire.

MAJOR PENSION SCANDALS

A number of pension scandals have shaken public confidence in recent years.

MAXWELL
In 1991, it was discovered that Robert Maxwell, head of the Mirror Group Newspapers business empire, had stolen £450 million from his employees' pension funds. Some money was recovered but many employees were left with reduced pensions. The scandal led to changes in pension legislation and the setting up of a scheme to compensate future pension scheme members who lose rights due to fraud.

EQUITABLE LIFE
During the 1950s Equitable began selling pension plans which guaranteed customers a minimum level of income from their annuities when they started to draw their pension. Equitable did not foresee or make provision for the growing cost of honouring these guarantees. By the 1990s the guarantees had become too expensive and Equitable sought to cut back the pay-out to the customers holding guaranteed annuities. The House of Lords ruled the cutbacks illegal and Equitable, faced with a gaping hole in its finances, closed its doors to new business. Many customers remain trapped and are getting poor returns on their pension schemes and other policies.

PENSIONS MIS-SELLING
In the late 1980s up to the mid-1990s, many people who belonged to occupational pension schemes were wrongly persuaded by financial advisers to switch to personal pensions even though they offered inferior pensions and other benefits. The regulator for the industry ordered a review which took several years but eventually over 1.1 million customers received over £10 billion in compensation.

SCHEMES WINDING UP WHERE THE EMPLOYER IS INSOLVENT
In the early 2000s, there was a spate of schemes winding up with too little in the pension fund to pay all the promised pensions. Normally the employer should have stepped in to make good the shortfall, but where the employer was insolvent, there was no-one to bale out the scheme. It is estimated that, as a result, some 85,000 scheme members lost substantial amounts of their promised pension, with at least 35,000 of these losing a half or more. The government has set up an assistance scheme to help these members (though some experts say the help is too little). The scandal also led to the setting up of a compensation scheme to help pension scheme members should they in future find themselves in a similar situation.

PERSONAL PENSIONS

Personal pensions are by their nature risky in the sense that you cannot know how much pension you will eventually get and you are exposed to the ups and downs of the investment markets. In general, there is no protection against these risks, but you can lessen and manage them as described in Chapter 9.

There are other types of risk that you can expect to be protected against, for example, being mis-sold a scheme which is unsuitable for you or losing your money through fraud.

How you are protected

Nearly all personal pensions come within the scope of the Financial Services Authority (FSA). The FSA is a body given powers by Parliament to regulate a very wide range of financial firms in the UK. In general, it is illegal for a firm to offer personal pensions to UK customers without being 'authorised' by the FSA. Provided you deal only with authorised firms, you can be confident that:

- The firm is solvent and run by people who appear to be honest.
- The personnel have at least a minimum level of training or are supervised.
- The business is run in accordance with rules set by the FSA. These include being open with you about the services it offers and their cost, providing you with key information about the firm's products and keeping proper records.
- If the firm is offering advice, the advice must be based on knowledge of you and your circumstances and be suitable advice.
- The firm must have a proper complaints procedure for you to use if things go wrong and belong to an independent complaints body (see pages 203-4).
- The firm is covered by the Financial Services Compensation Scheme (FSCS).

The Financial Services Compensation Scheme (FSCS)

If you lose money because of the negligence or dishonesty of a financial firm, you would normally claim redress from the firm using the complaints procedures described on page 203. But if the firm has become insolvent, this will not be possible. In that case, the FSCS may step in and provide compensation instead. Compensation is capped at a maximum amount – see the table below – which varies according to the way your money is invested. Most personal pensions offered by insurance companies technically count as insurance policies and so qualify for the higher level of compensation. The scheme is funded by a levy paid by authorised firms.

Self-invested personal pensions

Although most of the firms providing the investments you hold within a SIPP must be authorised by the FSA, the SIPP wrapper itself does not at the time of writing come within the scope of the FSA's regulation and nor do some investments such as direct holdings of commercial property. This means that if you have problems with, say, the administration of your SIPP, you would not necessarily have access to a complaints or compensation scheme. The government is proposing to change the law so that in future (probably from 2007) all SIPP providers will have to be authorised.

Maximum compensation available from the FSCS

Type of investment	Compensation limit	Maximum pay-out
Deposits	100% of first £2,000 90% of next £33,000	£31,700
Investments (for example, unit trusts and investment trusts)	100% of first £30,000 90% of next £20,00	£48,000
Long-term insurance (personal pensions, life insurance and annuities)	100% of the first £2,000 90% of remainder	Unlimited

WHAT TO DO IF YOU HAVE A COMPLAINT

Problems often stem from misunderstanding, so be prepared to work through an issue patiently, starting with the person or firm you originally dealt with. If that doesn't resolve the matter, there are independent complaints bodies which can help.

State pensions

During the years you are building up your state pension, you will be dealing with HM Revenue & Customs (regarding payment of National Insurance) and The Pension Service (concerning your state pension forecasts).

If you have problems with the Revenue, first contact the office you normally deal with. If you need to take the matter further ask to be put in touch with that office's Customer Relations Manager or Complaints Manager. If that still does not resolve the matter, contact the Director responsible for the office – you can find the address in the Revenue leaflet COP1 *Putting things right. How to complain* available from HM Revenue & Customs (www.hmrc.gov.uk).

If you are not happy with the Director's response, you can take your complaint to the Adjudicator's Office (www.adjudicatorsoffice.gov.uk). This is an independent body which can deal with complaints about mistakes, delays, misleading advice, staff behaviour and the Revenue's use of its discretionary powers.

Similarly, first contact The Pension Service department dealing with pension forecasts if you have a problem in this area. If necessary, ask for the contact details for the relevant Pension Centre Manager. If the problem persists, you can contact The Pension Service Chief Executive.

If, having exhausted these complaints procedures, you are still unhappy with the way the Revenue or The Pension Service have dealt with you, try contacting your Member of Parliament who can refer your case to the Parliamentary and Health Service Ombudsman (www.ombudsman.org.uk). The Ombudsman investigates maladministration by government departments. You cannot complain direct to the Ombudsman and must go through your MP.

Occupational schemes

Initially contact the pensions administrator for your scheme. If the problem is not resolved, say that

 If the firm that sold you the pension cannot resolve the problem, contact the Financial Ombudsman Service, www.financial-ombudsman.org.uk, tel: 0845 080 1800.

Planning points

Always keep a record of phone calls and correspondence regarding your pensions, noting the date, who you dealt with and the key points covered. These records will be important if later you have a dispute.

Preferably complain in writing as this provides a clear, unambiguous record of what you have said. Head your letter, fax or email 'Complaint'. Quote any relevant reference numbers so that your case can be easily traced. Be clear, concise and polite. State all relevant events, giving dates and if relevant the people involved. Spell out clearly the response you are seeking to resolve the matter.

can make judgments which are binding on both you and the pension scheme and can order the scheme to pay redress if appropriate up to £100,000.

Instead of going to the Ombudsman, you could go to court, but this will be a lengthy and expensive process.

Personal pensions

Complain first to the firm with whom you have a problem. All firms authorised by the FSA must have a formal complaints procedure. If you are uncertain of your rights or need support making your case to the firm, TPAS may be able to help.

you want to use the formal complaints procedure, which all occupational schemes must have and must give you details about. If this does not produce a satisfactory outcome, then take your complaint to The Pensions Advisory Service (TPAS) – (website www.pensionsadvisoryservice.org.uk).

TPAS is an independent mediation service. It can investigate your case and help you and your scheme to reach agreement. If that doesn't work, you can take your complaint to the Pensions Ombudsman. The services of TPAS and the Ombudsman are both free to complainants.

You must have gone through TPAS before the Ombudsman will consider your case. The Ombudsman

❝ The services of The Pensions Advisory Service and the Pensions Ombudsman are both free to complainants. ❞

Provided you have exhausted the firm's complaints procedure, if you are still unhappy, you can take your case to the Financial Ombudsman Service (FOS) (www.financial-ombudsman.org.uk).

The FOS is free to complainants. It will investigate your case and can make orders which are binding on the firm (but not you) to put the matter right. Where appropriate, FOS can order the firm to pay redress up to £100,000.

Free leaflets if you have a complaint

Reference	Title	From
COP1	Putting things right. How to complain	HM Revenue & Customs
AO1	The Adjudicator's Office for complaints about HM Revenue & Customs and Valuation Office Agency	Adjudicator's Office
GL22	Tell us how to improve our service	The Pension Service
	The Parliamentary Ombudsman How to complain to the Ombudsman	Parliamentary and Health Service Ombudsman
	The Pensions Advisory Service and the Pensions Ombudsman	Pensions Advisory Service
	Pensions dispute procedure	Pensions Advisory Service
	Personal pension problems?	Pensions Advisory Service
	Your complaint and the Ombudsman	Financial Ombudsman Service

❝ The Financial Ombudsman Service will investigate your case and can make orders which are binding on the firm (but not you) to put the matter right. ❞

Commonly, complaints to the ombudsman concern advice, for example, failing to explain the risks of income withdrawal.

If you are unhappy with the FOS decision, you have the option to take your case to court, but this could be a lengthy and expensive process. The FOS is able to make decisions that go beyond the strict legal position and take into account other aspects, such as good industry practice. So, if FOS has not found in your favour, try to be realistic about your chances of winning before deciding to go to court.

Useful addresses

Accountant – to find one

Association of Chartered Certified
Accountants
29 Lincoln's Inn Fields
London WC2A 3EE
Tel: 0207 396 7000
www.acca.co.uk

Institute of Chartered Accountants in
England and Wales
PO Box 433
Moorgate Place
London EC2P 2BJ
Tel: 0207 920 8100
www.icaew.co.uk

Institute of Chartered Accountants in
Ireland
83 Pembroke Road
Dublin 4
Republic of Ireland
Tel: (00 353) 1 637 7200
www.icai.ie

Institute of Chartered Accountants of
Scotland
21 Haymarket Yards
Edinburgh EH12 5BH
Tel: 0131 347 0100
www.icas.org.uk

The Adjudicator's Office

Haymarket House, 28 Haymarket
London SW1Y 4SP
Tel: 020 7930 2292
www.adjudicatorsoffice.gov.uk

Age equality at work

www.dti.gov.uk/er/equality/age.htm
www.agepositive.gov.uk

Association of British Insurers

51 Gresham Street
London EC2V 7HQ
Tel: 020 7600 3333
www.abi.org.uk

Consulting actuary

Association of Consulting Actuaries
Warnford Court
29 Throgmorton Street
London EC2N 2AT
Tel: 020 7382 4594
www.aca.org.uk

Society of Pension Consultants
St Bartholomew House
92 Fleet Street
London EC4Y 1DG
Tel: 020 7353 1688
www.spc.uk.com

Court - going to

England & Wales:
www.hmcourts-service.gov.uk

Scotland: www.scotcourts.gov.uk

Northern Ireland: ww.courtsni.gov.uk

Department for Work and Pensions (DWP)

DWP benefits for people of working age are administered through Jobcentre Plus. State pensions are administered by The Pension Service.
www.dwp.gov.uk

Ethical Investment Research Information Service (EIRIS)

80-84 Bondway
London SW8 1SF
Tel: 020 7840 5700
www.eiris.org

Financial Assistance Scheme (FAS)

The trustees of your pension scheme contact the FAS
Tel: 0845 601 9941
www.dwp.gov.uk/fas

Financial Ombudsman Service (FOS)

South Quay Plaza
183 Marsh Wall
London E14 9SR
Tel: 0845 080 1800
www.financial-ombudsman.org.uk

Financial Services Authority (FSA)

25 The North Colonnade
London E14 5HS
Tel: 020 7066 1000
www.fsa.gov.uk

FSA Consumer Helpline:
0845 6061234

FSA Register:
Consumer Helpline as above or
www.fsa.gov.uk/register

Consumer website:
http://www.fsa.gov.uk/consumer

Comparative tables:
http://www.fsa.gov.uk/tables

Financial Services Compensation Scheme (FSCS)

7th Floor
Lloyds Chambers
1 Portsoken Street
London E1 8BN
Tel: 020 7892 7300
www.fscs.org.uk

Fraud Compensation Fund

Knollys House
17 Addiscombe Road
Croydon
Surrey CR0 6SR
Tel: 0845 600 2541
www.pensionprotectionfund.org.uk

HM Revenue & Customs

For local tax enquiry centres look in the phonebook under 'HM Revenue & Customs' or the department's former name, 'Inland Revenue'.

For your local tax office, check your tax return, other tax correspondence or check with your employer or scheme paying you a pension.
www.hmrc.gov.uk

Independent financial adviser (IFA)

For a list of IFAs in your area, contact these organisations:

IFA Promotion
Tel: 0800 085 3250
www.unbiased.co.uk

The Institute of Financial Planning
Whitefriars Centre
Lewins Mead
Bristol BS1 2NT
Tel: 0117 945 2470
www.financialplanning.org.uk

MyLocalAdviser
www.mylocaladviser.com

The Personal Finance Society
20 Aldermanbury
London EC2V 7HY
Tel: 020 8530 0852
www.thepfs.org.uk

Independent financial advisers specialising in annuities

The Annuity Bureau
Alexander Forbes House
6 Bevis Marks
London EC3A 7AF
Tel: 0845 602 6263
www.annuity-bureau.co.uk

Annuity Direct
32 Scrutton Street
London EC2A 4RQ
Tel: 0500 50 65 75
www.annuitydirect.co.uk

Hargreaves Lansdown Annuity Supermarket
www.hlannuity.co.uk

WBA Ltd
Tel: 020 7421 4545
www.williamburrows.com

Jobcentre Plus
See phonebook for local office
www.jobcentreplus.gov.uk

Member of Parliament – to find your local MP

Your local public reference library or town hall.

House of Commons
Westminster
London SW1 0AA
Tel: 020 7219 4272
www.locata.co.uk/commons

Money Management

Magazine, available in larger newsagents
Subscriptions and back issues:
020 8606 7545

Moneyfacts

Moneyfacts House
66–70 Thorpe Road
Norwich
NR1 1BJ
Subscriptions: 0870 2250 100
www.moneyfacts.co.uk
Faxback services for pension annuities
(calls charged at maximum of 75p per
minute): 090 607 607 31

Money Observer

Magazine, available in newsagents
Subscriptions: 0870 870 1324
www.moneyobserver.net

NICO Contributor Group

National Insurance Contributions Office
Benton Park View
Newcastle upon Tyne
NE98 1ZZ
Tel: 0845 302 1479
www.hmrc.gov.uk/nic/aboutus.htm

Parliamentary and Health Service Ombudsman

To use this complaints service, contact
your MP:
Millbank Tower
Millbank
London
SW1P 4QP
Tel: 0845 015 4033
www.ombudsman.org.uk

Pension Calculator

www.pensioncalculator.org.uk

Pension centre

To find your local pension centre, see
phonebook or use search facility at
www.thepensionservice.gov.uk

Pension Protection Fund

Knollys House
17 Addiscombe Road
Croydon
Surrey CR0 6SR
Tel: 0845 600 2541
www.pensionprotectionfund.org.uk

Pension scheme administrator

See scheme handbook, recent benefit
statement, annual report or noticeboard
at work for contact details of pension
scheme administrator or trustees.
Alternatively, contact your personnel
department.

The Pension Service

Tel: 0845 60 60 265
www.thepensionservice.gov.uk

To get a state pension forecast:
Future Pension Centre (FPC)
The Pension Service
Tyneview Park
Whitley Road
Newcastle upon Tyne NE98 1BA
Tel: 0845 3000 168

To complain if pension centre has been unable to resolve matter:
Chief Executive
The Pension Service
PO Box 50101
London SW1P 2WU

Pension Tracing Service

The Pension Service
Tyneview Park
Whitley Road
Newcastle upon Tyne NE98 1BA
www.thepensionservice.gov.uk

The Pensions Advisory Service (TPAS)

11 Belgrave Road
London SW1V 1RB
Tel: 0845 601 2923
www.pensionsadvisoryservice.org.uk

Pensions Management

Subscriptions and back copies:
020 8606 7545
www.pensions-management.co.uk

Pensions Ombudsman

11 Belgrave Road
London SW1V 1RB
Tel: 020 7834 9144
www.pensions-ombudsman.org.uk

Pensions Regulator

Napier House
Trafalgar Place
Brighton BN1 4DW
Tel: 0870 606 3636
www.thepensionsregulator.gov.uk

Resolution (formerly Solicitors' Family Law Association)

PO Box 302
Orpington
Kent BR6 8QX
Tel: 01689 820272
www.resolution.org.uk

Standard & Poors

www.funds-sp.com

State pension age calculator

www.thepensionservice.gov.uk/resourcec
entre/home/statepensioncalc.asp

Tax office

See entry above for HM Customs & Excise

TrustNet

www.trustnet.com

Glossary

Accrual rate In a salary-related pension scheme, the proportion of your pay that you get as pension for each year you have been in the scheme.

Active fund management Trying to improve the returns from an investment fund by constantly monitoring and trading the underlying investments in an attempt to pick the best performers.

Actuarial reduction A cut in your pension if you retire early to reflect the extra cost of paying your pension for longer. Often 6 per cent for each year of early retirement.

Actuary Financial and statistical expert who uses mathematical techniques to estimate how the future may turn out. With pension schemes, actuaries design schemes and advise on issues, such as, the expected size of future benefits and level of contributions needed to ensure those benefits can be paid.

Alternatively secured pension (ASP) A type of income withdrawal from age 75 where the maximum pension you can draw is based on cautious assumptions to guard against your pension fund running out during your lifetime and other restrictions apply.

Annual limit for relief The maximum contributions you can make to pension schemes each year which qualify for tax relief. The limit is £3,600 or, if higher, your total earnings for the year.

Annuity Investment where you swap a lump sum (such as a pension fund) for an income either for life or a specified number of years. You can't get your money back as a lump sum.

Annuity rate The amount of pension you get in return for your lump sum.

Assumption An educated guess which may turn out to be right or wrong.

Authorised Means a firm has been checked out by the Financial Services Authority and is allowed to conduct financial business in the UK. Provided you deal with an authorised firm, you benefit from consumer protection – for example, complaints procedures and a compensation scheme if things go wrong.

Benefit statement A statement issued by a pension scheme showing the amount of pension you might get at a specified age based on the amount of pension built up so far, the amount you might continue to build up if contributions are still being paid in, and various assumptions.

Bond A loan to either a government or a company which can be bought and sold on a stock market.

Capital The amount of money you originally invest.

Capital risk The likelihood of losing part or all of your original investment and/or gains you have already built up.

Cash balance scheme Type of pension scheme that promises you a set amount of pension fund at retirement for each year you have been in the scheme. The pension you get then depends on how much pension you can buy with fund.

Civil partner Since 5 December 2005, same-sex couples have been able to register their relationship as a civil partnership and, for most purposes, are then treated in the same way as husbands and wives.

Commutation The process of swapping part of your retirement pension for a tax-free lump sum.

Commutation factor The amount of tax-free lump sum you get for each £1 a year of pension you give up.

Contracted out Describes the situation where instead of building up state additional pension, a person is saving for retirement through an occupational pension scheme or a personal pension. Some of the National Insurance contributions that would normally have gone towards the additional pension are used instead to provide benefits from the occupational scheme or personal pension.

Contracting out Giving up some state additional pension and building up a pension instead through either an occupational scheme or a personal pension/stakeholder scheme. Part of the National Insurance you and your employer pay which would have gone towards the state scheme is used to build up the alternative pension.

Contribution Money paid into a pension scheme by you or someone else, for example, your employer.

Contributory scheme Pension scheme to which you are required to pay contributions.

Defined benefit scheme Type of pension scheme that promises you a set level of pension typically based on your pay and length of time in the scheme.

Equities Another name for shares in companies.

Financial Services Authority (FSA) Body established by law to regulate the provision of, and advice about, most financial products and services in the UK. It also publishes a wide range of information in print and on its website at www.fsa.gov.uk.

FTSE 100 Index A measure of stock market performance based on the share prices of the 100 largest companies quoted on the London Stock Exchange.

Gilts The name for bonds issued by the UK government.

Gross An amount before deduction of tax or tax relief. It equals the net amount plus the tax or tax relief deducted.

Inflation A sustained rise in the price level. In the UK, inflation is usually measured as the change in the Retail Prices Index (RPI). The RPI is based on the prices of a large basket of goods and services, typical of the items which the average household buys.

Investment fund A wide range of different shares and/or other investments chosen by a fund manager. The investments are purchased by pooling your money with that of lots of other investors.

Joint-life-last-survivor annuity An investments where you exchange a lump sum (say, your pension fund) for an income payable until both you and your partner have died. You can choose whether or not the income reduces following the first death.

Life expectancy The number of years a person of a certain age is expected to live.

Life expectancy The number of years someone of a given age is on average expected to live based on statistical evidence.

Longevity The propensity to live a long time. When longevity is increasing, people tend to live longer than in the past.

Lower earnings limit (LEL) The lowest level of earnings which count towards the record on which certain state benefits, such as your state pension, are based.

Means-tested state benefit Income from the state where the amount you get depends on the level of your income from other sources (and, in some cases, also your savings). An example is pension credit.

Money purchase scheme Type of pension scheme where the pension you get depends on the amount paid in, how well the invested contributions grow and the amount of pension you can buy at retirement with the resulting fund.

National Insurance contributions A tax paid by most people who work. There are different types of contribution, called 'classes'. Paying some classes of contribution entitles you to claim state benefits, such as state retirement pension.

Net An amount after deduction of tax or tax relief.

NICO Stands for National Insurance Contributions Office, the part of HM Revenue & Customs that deals with the collection and recording of National Insurance contributions.

Non-contributory scheme Pension scheme where you pay no contributions and your employer bears the full cost of the scheme.

Open market option Your option to shop around and buy an annuity from any provider of your choice rather than sticking with the provider with whom you have built up your pension fund.

Passive fund management Setting up an investment fund to mimic the performance of a stock market index.

Pension fund A pool of investments into which contributions are paid and which is used to provide pensions and other pension scheme benefits as they fall due for payment.

Pensionable earnings The definition of pay used by a salary-related scheme when working out the pension it will pay and for setting contributions.

Preserved pension The pension you are promised at normal pension age from a scheme you have left.

Primary threshold The level of earnings at which employees (and their employers) start to pay National Insurance contributions.

Private sector The part of the economy which is independent of the state.

Prohibited assets Residential property and possessions such as cars, fine wines, art and antiques. Self-directed pension schemes are taxed prohibitively if they invest in these assets.

Public sector The part of the economy to do with the state. For example, public sector workers are people employed by central or local government or state services such as the National Health Service. They include, for example, NHS staff, teachers, firemen, police.

Purchased life annuity An annuity you choose to buy with money other than a pension fund. Part of each payment you receive counts as return of your original investment and is tax-free. The rest is taxable.

Qualifying year A tax year which counts towards your state basic pension because you have paid or been credited with enough National Insurance contributions.

Reference scheme A notional pension scheme with pension and other benefits that set the minima which a contracted-out salary-related scheme must match.

Registered pension scheme A scheme designed to provide a pension and often other benefits too (such as life cover and pensions for survivors if you die) which qualifies for advantageous tax treatment.

Retirement Used in this book to mean the period of life when you draw a pension. You might not have stopped work altogether.

Section 32 scheme A pension scheme offered by insurance companies. It is designed to accept preserved pension rights from an occupational scheme and can maintain them in their original form (say, salary-related).

Self-directed pension scheme A scheme where you choose the specific investments the fund invests in. The main examples are self-invested personal pensions (SIPPs) and small self-administered schemes (SSASs).

Shares An investment that makes you a part-owner of a company along with all the other shareowners. The return you get depends on how well the company performs.

Short-term annuity An investment where you swap a lump sum for an income paid out for a specified period of time. At the end of the period, the income stops. You cannot normally get your original investment back as lump sum.

Single life annuity An investment where you exchange a lump sum (say, your pension fund) for an income payable for as long as you live.

Sponsoring employer The employer who sets up and contributes to an occupational scheme.

State basic pension Part of the state pension which nearly everyone gets.

State pension age Age at which you become eligible to claim your state pension. Currently 65 for men and 60 for women.

Tax deferral Putting off a tax bill until a later time. This could save tax if your tax rate in future is lower than now.

Tax month A month running from the sixth day of one month to the fifth day of the next, for example 6 April to 5 March. Tax months are used in relation to both tax and state benefits.

Tax relief A reduction in tax given either as a deduction from your tax bill or by reducing the amount you pay towards things that qualify for the relief (such as pension contributions).

Tax year A period of a year running from 6 April to the following 5 April. For example, '2006-7' means the year from 6 April 2006 to 5 April 2007. Generally, both taxes and state benefits are set in relation to tax years.

Taxable Describes income or gains on which you may have to pay tax depending on your personal circumstances.

Today's money The amount of money you would need today to be worth the same in terms of what it might buy as a sum of money that you will get at some time in the future. For example £100 in ten years' time would be worth £50 in today's money if prices doubled over the ten-year period.

Transfer value The lump sum which, if invested now, is deemed to be enough to provide a given level of pension at retirement plus other benefits. This cash sum can be transferred from one scheme to another.

Upper earnings limit (UEL) The highest level of earnings which count towards the record on which your state pension is based.

Working life The tax years from the one in which you reach age 16 to the last complete tax year before you reach state pension age.

Working tax credit A state benefit for people who are in work but on a low income.

Index

Index

Index

Index

Which? is the leading independent consumer champion in the UK.
A not-for-profit organisation, we exist to make individuals as powerful as the
organisations they deal with in everyday life. The next few pages give you a
taster of our many products and services. For more information, log onto
www.which.co.uk or call 0800 252 100.

Make life better with Which?

Now you've found the information in the Pensions Handbook of great value,
why not join us and have Which? magazine delivered to your door every month?
From saving money on your bills to balancing your investment portfolio, it's got
all you need to sort out your finances and keep them in order long-term.

But Which? isn't just about managing your money. We can help with all your
spending decisions too. Whether you're looking for a widescreen TV, a digital
camera or a new car (not forgetting a kettle or toaster, of course!) our renowned
and totally independent Which? Best Buys are the shortcut you need to find the
very best product at the very best price.

And we'll keep you up to date with all the latest consumer news that affects
you too.

But your subscription gets you much more than just a magazine. You'll be part
of an organisation that campaigns to get a fairer deal for all consumers. And our
members' website has all the latest test results and buying guides for everything
from washing machines to credit cards.

Whatever we're testing, Which? is always on your side. We're impartial, unbiased
and we don't take advertising so you can trust us to give you an honest opinion.
And we do!

Get the best out of life with Which? magazine. To take out a trial subscription call
us on 0800 252100 or visit www.which.co.uk

Which? - The most trusted magazine in the UK

Which? Online

www.which.co.uk gives you access to all Which? content online. It's updated daily, so you can read hundreds of product reports and Best Buy recommendations, keep up to date with Which? campaigns, compare products, use our financial planning tools and interactive car-buying guide. You can also access all the reviews from the *The Which? Good Food Guide*, ask an expert in our interactive forums, register for e-mail updates and browse our online shop – so what are you waiting for? www.which.co.uk.

Which? Legal Service

Which? Legal Service offers immediate access to first-class legal advice at unrivalled value. One low-cost annual subscription allows members to enjoy unlimited legal advice by telephone on a wide variety of legal topics, including consumer law (problems with goods and services), employment law, holiday problems, neighbour disputes and parking/speeding/clamping issues. Our qualified lawyers help members reach the best outcome in a user-friendly way, guiding them through each stage on a step-by-step basis. Call 0800 252 100 for more information or visit www.which.co.uk.

Computing Which?

If you own a computer, are thinking of buying one or just want to keep abreast of the latest technology and keep up with your kids, there's one invaluable source of information you can turn to – *Computing Which?* magazine. *Computing Which?* offers you honest unbiased reviews of the best (and worst) new technology, invaluable problem-solving tips from the experts and step-by-step guides to help you make the most of your computer. To subscribe, call 0800 252 100 and quote 'Computing' or go to www.computingwhich.co.uk.

which?

Which? Books

Which? Books provide impartial, expert advice on everyday matters from finance to law, property to major life events. We also publish the country's most trusted restaurant guide, *The Which? Good Food Guide*. To find out more about Which? Books, log on to www.which.co.uk or call 01903 828557.

Other books in this series

Which? Essential Guides
Buying Property Abroad

Jeremy Davies
ISBN: 1-84490-024-X/978-1844-900-244

A complete guide to the legal, financial and practical aspects of buying property abroad. This book provides down-to-earth advice on how the buying process differs from the UK, and how to negotiate contracts, commission surveys, and employ lawyers and architects. Practical tips on currency deals and taxes – and how to command the best rent – all ensure you can buy abroad with total peace of mind.

Which? Essential Guides
Buy, Sell and Move House

Kate Faulkner
ISBN: 1-844900-26-6/978-1844-900-266

A complete, no-nonsense guide to negotiating the property maze and making your move as painless as possible. From dealing with estate agents to chasing solicitors, working out the true cost of your move to understanding Home Information Packs, this guide tells you how to keep things on track and avoid painful sticking points.

" Which? tackles the issues that really matter to consumers and gives you the advice and active support you need to buy the right products. "